The Shy Writer

The Shy Writer

An Introvert's Guide to Writing Success

Written By
C. Hope Clark

FundsforWriters
First printing 2004.

ISBN – 1-59113-583-4

ATTENTION BUSINESSES, UNIVERSITIES, COLLEGES, HIGH SCHOOLS and PROFESSIONAL ORGANIZATIONS: Contact either Booklocker.com or author C. Hope Clark for discounts on bulk purchases of this book for educational needs, gift purposes, or as premiums for increasing subscriptions or renewals. Contact Booklocker.com or C. Hope Clark at hope@fundsforwriters.com.

SUBSCRIBE TO FUNDSFORWRITERS NEWSLETTERS ONLINE http://www.FundsforWriters.com.

Dedication

To the quiet souls tapping reclusive keyboards and living through their words and visions.

To FundsforWriters fans who allow me to live through my words and give me vision.

To a husband who understands my passion to write and loves me for being me.

To sons who brag about their writer mom yet kid me for not making millions.

To parents who taught me that the right priorities in life are those that make you a better person.

Table of Contents

About the Author and FundsforWriters

Cynthia Hope Beales Clark, AKA C. Hope Clark, was born in a little town called Rolling Fork, Mississippi in October 19__ ...wait – scratch this! First, you do not care about it, and second, you do not need to know my age. We are not that friendly yet.

But...by the time you get to the end of this book, I want you to feel like you know me. I hope you feel that we have had a nice long chat about how to deal with your writing, your promotion, your shyness, and your self-esteem. Sense of familiarity and community of belonging is a trademark of FundsforWriters.

I started writing articles and giving advice on finding funds after speaking to a group of women about writing for the Internet. But the writing topic rapidly detoured to the subject of finding the financial means to write. I rode home from Atlanta, Georgia to Columbia, South Carolina that night with my mind whirling. Here I thought writers spent every waking moment weaving tales when instead they needed money for computers, ink, postage, and gasoline. My romantic visions of writers crumbled around the edges when I realized the agonies of real, everyday writers.

At that time I worked within the federal government and spent my career advising people about financial affairs. I dealt with the rural underprivileged: farmers, businesses, small communities, and even other government agencies, assisting them with finding funds. Surely I could use that knowledge to help individual writers.

Before long I was up to my elbows in newsletters, research, and business cards. That was early 2000. The chat I had with twelve women in the back room of a bookstore evolved to 9500+ writers nationwide with a few sprinkled around the globe. Hopefully and most likely, by the time you pick up this book, the number will have grown again. And I so love these writers.

FundsforWriters is the personality of C. Hope Clark. FFW offers current deadlines and detailed listings of contests, awards, jobs, freelance markets, grants, and publishers to writers who do not have the time or the know-how to find them. Cynthia Brian, founder of Starstyle Productions ® and Be the Star You Are ®, nicknamed me "Freelance Hope" because she envisioned me in that light – providing hope for freelance writers everywhere. After 25 years as an actor, director, producer and designer in the entertainment business and as a current coach, consultant, and motivational speaker, she seemed pretty adamant about that picture. Who was I to argue? The words follow my signature today.

FundsforWriters and Freelance Hope work unilaterally to educate and motivate writers struggling with the business side of writing. FFW works through positive and uplifting messages not only to inspire writers, but also to better educate them toward success. Writers work damn hard for the money they make. Who else would work that hard for so little unless they adored what they were doing? That is why FFW defines success as *making a living doing what you love* – not necessarily being rich. Whether paying for a one bedroom flat or a two-story waterfront chateau, the writing income starts by learning how to manage time, promote your work wisely, and follow through on opportunities. Submit, submit, submit is a mantra that pays off in the long run. If you become wealthy along the way, that's great, but the wealth is not the focal point. Passion fulfilled is true measure of success.

FundsforWriters is a website, a family of newsletters, several ebooks and now books about developing ways to live the writing life. It's a voice that nurtures, scolds, and coaxes writers struggling to dream. Nothing soothes the soul more than living a dream, and to a writer that means penning words often and reading bylines plenty. Doing that for life can surely help one live and die happy.

Preface

Her pillow absorbed the flow of tears. No matter how she rested her head on the sham, she tasted salt and stuck to wet cotton. Throwing it on the floor, she put her cheek on the cool, dry mattress and sucked in sporadic, shallow breaths, exhausted from the crying and the effort to hide it. For the fifth night, she retreated to bed to release the tension she hid by day. The recital was a week away and regardless of how much she practiced, she missed a note at least every third run through the piece. She knew that a thousand eyes would watch her fingers, a thousand ears would hear her notes, and a pair of parents would expect perfection from her. Right before exhaustion put her to sleep, she pondered how much it would hurt to break her arm over the side of the bathtub and if she had the guts to do it.

Shyness is painful. I am a shy person. And I was that little girl at age 13 right before a piano recital. I enjoyed the piano. My teacher felt I had talent. And I rehearsed my music for hours at a time until I know my daddy wanted to scream. But I despised recitals to the point they almost made me sick.

Most writers have a tendency toward reclusive behavior. Nothing inspires me more than several days of pure solitude allowing me to write myself silly. Even the dogs get bored with my hermitic desires. My husband works late and I don't complain, because the extra hour or two means I can start another article or add the finishing touches to a chapter.

One-on-one I'm spontaneous, articulate, and able to improvise. But a room full of people unleashes internal butterflies, churns my stomach, and accelerates my pulse with the ultimate need being a trip to the bathroom where I wonder why I don't have to pee when I thought I did.

Over the years, I learned to hide the fear. I have a real clever façade that reeks of confidence, but once I'm out of the environment and away from all those eyes, I decompress. I can literally feel my shoulder muscles relax as I drive away from the event. And when I go to sleep that night, I'm worn out from the pent up stress of the day.

Over the years, I developed some tricks to deal with the doubt, the apprehension, and the feeling of helplessness most people get when they step into the light, up on the stage, or out before an audience. I can even volunteer to speak if it means more sales or there is no other alternative. But believe me, if I can find a different route other than standing in front of people, I will capitalize upon it.

If you've picked up this book, you have a fear as well. Or else you desire to help someone who has that fear. This is not a book to make you enjoy speaking and putting on a show in front of strangers. This is a book to help you deal with shyness within the writing world in your own fashion. You do not have to speak at conferences. You do not have to be embarrassed at a book signing. You do not have to hawk your product and feel like a used-car salesman. Or you might have a desire to do all these things but do not know how to start. Your personality is your personality. You write because it meshes well with your character. You do not have to sacrifice yourself to fit someone else's mold of a writer. Challenge is good for growth, but agony is unhealthy. The comfort level is yours to find.

Here you receive pointers on how to maneuver in the writing arena without the social weight around your neck. And you will learn how to manage during times when you absolutely have to make appearances you cannot dodge. What you won't receive is a message telling you to "get over it." While Toastmasters is educational and worthwhile, it is not the cure-all. If you are shy and don't want to "get over it," this is the book for you.

"To begin with, you must know what you want."
~*Mary Kay Ash*

Chapter 1
Understanding Shyness

- Your Hair Color
- Super Hero Syndrome
- Labels
- Introverts vs. Extroverts
- Your Comfort Level

Your heart races, banging against your ribs, your chest, your throat. Fingers grip a pen to disguise the shake. The other hand flattens on your leg, your side, and your leg again drying the moisture that never disappears. You did not bargain for exhibition when you entered the world of writing. What started as a reclusive haven for your creative muse evolved into a public forum to sell your work. Good work should sell itself, you say...you wish.

You read the lists, blogs and newsletters about making a living at a craft that requires hours of quiet time. We hear the stories about writers who self-publish to hold a book in their hands only to learn that selling it is a whole other issue. How-to books deny that writers are generally a reclusive lot, but face it, the majority of writers love to write, hate to sell, and wish the world would encroach only when beckoned.

I firmly believe that some writers quit writing because of the pageantry of marketing, and as one of those leery about staring at a roomful of people examining my hair and clothes, I felt some sense of salvation necessary. The genuinely shy writer needs relief from such public scrutiny, whether from the masses or the few. After experiencing the agony of publicity and witnessing two-hour book signings where bookstore employees outnumbered the attendees, I decided writers everywhere needed a reprieve.

So you're painfully shy? Hope still flickers. You can dodge the public's eye and still remain successful as a writer. Just change your strategy and get savvy at behind-the-scenes planning.

Your Hair Color

Other sources advise you how to get over it, as if you wanted to. Shyness is a personal trait, and many people have no desire to overcome an inherent part of their personal composition. Social phobia is an extreme version of shyness, which requires assistance and training to overcome, occasionally with medication. But nervousness and an uncomfortable feeling in front of people is not a character flaw as many would like you to believe. It is as much a part of you as the real color of your hair.

Hmm...speaking of hair color, let's use that analogy. You have light brown hair. You hate it. You can't curl it, style it or cut it to your satisfaction and you assume others are not all that impressed either. So you put a little rinse on it and voila! You're a classy blonde. Nature gave you brown hair, but in the public's eye you glow blonde.

You are shy. Whether you like it or not, it can be an obstacle at times or even personally painful when you have no choice but to walk in front of people. But you have options – lots of options. You can "color" that shyness with a front of confidence. You can find other avenues to make a presentation without standing alone on a platform. You can create a gimmick that precedes you and makes the sale for you. You have all sorts of colors you can put on that shyness and feel good about yourself. But you always know what your natural hair color is and the type of person you truly are inside.

Yes, good work should sell itself, but in today's environment, hype and advertising sell products with quality taking a distant third behind packaging and gimmicks. The big publishing houses make contract decisions based upon projected sales, not literary strengths. The shy writer today is at a disadvantage in that regard unless her name is already famous as an actor, CEO, or comedian, but they are not our targeted market. We are concerned with you – the writer.

I won't lie to you...public speaking can enhance sales. The public wants to see and touch the gifted, and published writers fall within that category. Of course, these writers might be making all of $10,000 a year in royalties, but they published a book and that success is what others see.

For you to sell your writing, you have to decide:
1. Do you want to "get over" your shyness?
2. Do you want to disguise your shyness?
3. Do you want to leave well enough alone and deal from behind the shyness?

None of these decisions is wrong or right. Do not let finances be the only reason for making your choice. There are ways – lots of ways - to manage your shyness if you have grown quite fond of it, and you must decide what makes for a comfortable life for you as a writer. If it is a friend, keep it. If it is a foe, get rid of it.

You might have to read through the entire book to grasp where you stand. Change is not easy nor is it natural. But if you are hell-bent on building a new you, then jump in and start adjusting. If you are not so sure, take your time.

Super Hero Syndrome

I am a shy person. Some people who know me would agree – others think I am not. Some would call me downright cocky, while others know that my preference is a cabin in the pine-topped foothills of the Carolinas alone with my computer and Mother Nature. Of course, hubby can come along and the children can visit, but I never tire of solitude. Is that shy?

I worked for 25 years in the federal government where the public was my client. I met people daily who were dealing with private financial matters, unemployment, even foreclosure. After a few years I acquired the title of Boss, overseeing other managers, personnel issues, and budget dilemmas. The buck stopped on my desk a zillion times, usually requiring assertive behavior on my part to save someone's promotion, financial standing or even employment. I learned valuable lessons during those times by weighing the introvert versus the extrovert in me. The main lesson I learned was that when my behavior impacted someone else's life or livelihood, I traded my shyness for concern about him. Not a conscious effort, the shift from introvert to extrovert just happened. When I had the choice of getting involved or not, the innocent parties determined the extent of my active participation.

Let's call it the Super Hero Syndrome. Clark Kent and Peter Parker led docile lives with their costumes hidden. When thinking of themselves, they withdrew into their writing and photography (coincidental, huh?). But when others stood to be harmed, an alternate ego jumped forth as Superman and Spiderman. They were needed so they rose to the occasion and the shyness melted away.

That's how I deal with my shyness. I hate controversy. My mother will tell you I always have dodged controversy. But I deal with it when necessary. That dividing line is what you have to define. When is dealing with your shyness a necessity? Crossing that line is different for each person and once you understand that you develop a comfort level with your own character traits.

Labels

Often, people misconstrue shyness as other types of behavior. Shy people improperly receive labels such as:

- Insecure
- Unhappy
- Aloof
- Arrogant
- Devious
- Dumb
- Genius
- Anti-social

The general population likes quick labels. Why? Because people do not like uncertainty. Everyone wants to know who and what they are dealing with, and when faced with new people, they not only seek to put a name to a face, but they more quickly search for a comfort level with the strangers that wander into their world. You do it, too.

On the bus, you desperately want to know if the person seated next to you will pick your pocket or pose a threat, so you hold your purse a little tighter. With your guard up, you look for the ally and the foe from the first moment you report to work at a new job until labels are established. You wish for a banker you can trust with your private financial information and goodness knows it takes some soul searching to find a psychiatric or marriage counselor that fits seamlessly with your persona. And don't we discuss in chatrooms how literary agents must be perfect matches to capitalize on their services?

Before you label, you parley and dance with all the knowledge you can gather before allowing the person in. On the bus, you have limited time and little need to know the individual, so you make a judgment in a split second. A smell, a coat, a beard, bags under the eyes or dirt under the fingernails may tilt your decision one way or another. You have no need to query the person and breach your wall of shyness to reach a conclusion. So you keep to yourself; no one would blame you.

At work, however, you face the same people every day. You have more time but also you have more at stake. The wrong decision could mean being disliked by the boss or losing a project. Co-workers can erode your promotion or pave the way to it. Your veil of shyness slowly comes down, but only when the facts are laid before you. It may take a few weeks, but you eventually recognize the friends, the enemies and the neutrals you must meld into the 40 hours a week you call your second home.

As a writer, however, you are faced with a sea of strangers, often an invisible audience, all with potential to support you or tear you down. You usually cannot touch them or see them. You cannot identify them, but you know they are there. What you do impacts them, and they impact you in return. Stop and think...you are no different than the President of the United States, Oscar-winning actors, and Chief Executive Officers (CEOs). They serve the public and find their careers in the hands of thousands or even millions. A public job is an awesome responsibility and the intimidation is enough to make anyone retreat.

So how do they lighten that burden? They do a market study and learn more about whom they serve. They reach for the needs of the many to see how they can provide satisfaction. Call it public relations or market analysis, but they each can tell you the segments of the general population that support them, hate them, or do not care at all. Then they channel their attentions in the appropriate directions.

The President might be a Democrat. Those people put him in office. And while he serves all, he has marketing people that identify the types of voters that put him there and those that did not, and if the numbers are close, he learns to reach those on the fringes. He isn't going to make too many people change parties.

An actor specializes in comedic movies. Some viewers go to the theatre for drama, romance or even horror but care little for humor on the screen. Does that actor strive to reach those moviegoers or does he focus on the comedy fans in the world?

Many CEOs are marketing gurus. They know which segment of what population will buy so many widgets for how long and for what purpose. Full-time marketing experts channel constant feedback to the CEO so that the company directs its resources in the most efficient and effective direction.

You provide entertainment and education in your words to the world. You hopefully know the readers that fall into your genre. You know the professional groups, the editors, the publications, and the conferences that cater to you or pose as opportunity for your work. You need to have a serious feel for your readership. Your customers are your focus. With them you can lower a little bit of your guard.

Contained within those groups are the serious fans. If you do not have them yet, you will if you stick to writing. They buy the newspaper because of your column. They sign up for your newsletter to hear your op-ed. They lose themselves in your romance sagas, and feel goose bumps through your mysteries while looking forward to your next release. They identify with the little girl and her puppy in your children's book. Here is the ultimate shyness test. How much of yourself do you give to these people?

Introverts vs. Extroverts

The extrovert talks and talks and laughs and flaunts herself to her fans, potential fans, plus anyone else who will listen. She enjoys the limelight. The experts tell you that this type of person sells more books.

The introvert signs books and smiles and declines lone public appearances. He might sit on a panel at a conference but would lose his lunch if he had to speak alone. Book tours are not an option, and teaching a class is out of the question. The experts tell you that this type of person is less than successful.

Fact is, quiet and internally driven people process thoughts and information differently than the assertive and boisterous types. More and more studies prove that the two types possibly have different physiological make-ups. People draw out the strengths of extroverts. Calm introspection triggers the power of introverts.

Extroverts have no concept of how to deal with introverts. Energized by people and social situations, they thrive around human stimuli. If they cannot find people, they pick up the cell phone to reach someone for interaction. Extroverts want others to know all about them. They also enjoy the company of introverts because the extrovert thinks that these calm souls absorb everything being said.

Introverts, on the other hand, know everything about extroverts. How can they not when the person is spilling everything? There is nothing an introvert likes less than talking about himself. Introverts thoroughly enjoy the solitude and usually need a ratio of three to four hours of "downtime" alone to one hour with people to maintain a sense of sanity. Interaction with other people wears down introverts and drains them of the same energy that empowers extroverts. Solitude, on the other hand, recharges the introvert.

Dr. Carl Jung's theories about the dynamics of the psyche placed mankind on a continuum with extremes on either end. These dynamics became defined in three principles of opposites, equivalence, and entropy. Within this thought he created a personality typology that distinguished the difference between introversion and extroversion. Many people remember him for little else.

Extroverts enter publicly visual positions like politics, marketing and corporate management. Such individuals receive much attention and therefore they tend to set the standard and expectation for the average person. Since they are often seen and frequently followed by the press, the public interprets their success and actions as the right path to follow. Popularity breeds desire. An extrovert equates to "people person," an enviable trait in an interactive, competitive world. And this world interprets introverted as restricted, restrained and handicapped.

Jonathan Rauch wrote a column for the *Atlantic Monthly* in March 2003 entitled "Caring for Your Introvert." He described introverted personalities as repressed in today's society since extroverts dominate public forums. He quoted Calvin Coolidge as one of few introverted politicians, "Don't you know that four-fifths of all our troubles in this life would disappear if we would just sit down and keep still?"

As a quiet person how many times have you wished a group, room, or audience would just shut up? I have innumerable times. Noise irritates me. I love focus and concentration as do most shy writers. In the quiet lulls of life the shy find motivation, inspiration, and satisfaction. In my reading, research, and observation about these polar opposites, I find the internal thinkers are more intelligent as a whole, more refined, more sensible, and rather independent. Mr. Rauch pointed out that extroverts sometimes envision introverts as arrogant. "...it is probably due to our lack of small talk, a lack that extroverts often mistake for disdain. We tend to think before talking, whereas extroverts tend to think by talking, which is why their meetings never last less than six hours."

So are extroverts the most successful salespeople? Not necessarily. I have seen loud people sell little and insult many. And I have witnessed book signings where the quiet author sells out of autographed copies. The intensity of public display is not the driving factor of writing success. The quality of the message and the consistency of the delivery says it all and should be your foremost goal.

Your Comfort Level

In a few words...the successful writer fills a reader's need. And once you fill that need, those readers become fixed upon your product. They do not expect loud or soft words. They do not expect a fast talker or a slow presenter. They want satisfaction and your job is to produce.

If you can meet the needs of your readers from behind the scenes, then do it. If you need to step in front of a crowd, do it. And if you are ill from the effort, paralyzed by the fear, or nervous due to phobias, you will not meet the needs of your customers. They need to "see" your best side. If that means discarding the spotlighted book readings and avoiding live public appearances, then do so.

Writing is about the readers, but it is about the writers, too. The happy balance of pleasing the reader and enabling the writer is key to a fruitful career. An unhappy scribe is good for no one. Depressed novelists and suicidal poets make for interesting history, but today the point is to grab the gusto and enjoy life through the talents given you. Write with a passion, promote yourself by honoring your worth and remember that your readers want you to be a success. Sacrificing your personality in the process is not the answer. The shy writer in you has choices. Your job is to capitalize upon those choices and find the methods that work for you and your readers. Being shy is not a problem; it's who you are.

The indispensable first step to getting the things
you want out of life is this; decide what you want.

~ Ben Stein, Actor and Author

Chapter 2
Defining the Shyness

- The Grip of Shyness
- Tweaking Yourself
- Fight or Flight
- The Social Animal

Over half of the adult population claims shyness as a part of their lives. And the majority of the other half admits to shy phases in their lives. A measly 10% or so deny any evidence of shyness in their persona in the past or present. So why do people not want to be shy when it appears to be a natural occurrence?

Marti Olsen Laney, PsyD and author of *The Introvert Advantage: How to Thrive in an Extrovert World*, says, "Shyness is often confused with introversion but it is social anxiety, and either introverts or extroverts can be shy." Shy people retreat within themselves or compensate by stepping out and tackling the situation.

The public interprets shyness as a shortcoming and outgoing behavior as successful. They read shyness as a lack of confidence and outgoing behavior as control. It's all a game, people. Some of the extroverts are shy people. And some shy people are very self-assured, just not willing to flaunt.

All this second-guessing drives writers nuts when we ponder marketing our column, book, script or article. We must take command of ourselves to operate in the public domain and we must know how to manipulate or accommodate our clientele to make sales. Why can't we just be our natural selves?

Some people retain their shyness throughout their lives. Others outgrow it either through simple maturity or overt effort. But what helps you as a shy writer more than anything else is the identification of what makes you shy. And once you identify the behavior, situation or obstacle that aggravates that shyness, you open yourself to choices in dealing with the scenarios. When you define your parameters and limitations, you gain a comfort level and learn what to wrap your arms around. Putting a finger on your issue is half the battle and often acts as a magic spell, making part of the nervous behavior just go "poof" and blow away. If it doesn't, you learn to deal with it. And if the shy behavior is extremely difficult for you, learn to work around it.

The Grip of Shyness

Shyness is a desire to remain internal and avoid stepping forward. Some definitions add phrases like "interfere with the ability to enjoy one's self." Enjoying yourself is subjective, and the only person who can define that enjoyment is you. Read the characteristics below and try to understand what happens to you when shyness takes a grip:

Voice Issues
- Soft voice
- High pitched or squeaky voice
- Lisp, stutter, or enunciation
- Heavy accent
- Dry mouth
- Loss of voice
- Word stumbling
- Talk too fast or too slow

Fear Issues
- Forgetfulness
- Inappropriate laughter
- Nausea
- Rejection
- Depression
- Disappointment
- Pity
- Stupidity
- Opposition or controversy
- Eye contact

Appearance Issues
- Slouching
- Stumbling
- Hand shaking
- Sweaty hands or forehead

Physical ailments may be difficult to overcome but then again they might have simple solutions. A voice that quits unexpectedly is an uncertainty no one wishes. A pitch that does not carry well erodes confidence and causes the message to fade into thin air. Your heritage may cause audience difficulties in some regions due to your accent. And who wants to throw up in front of strangers, fans, or customers?

Maybe you have a physical trait you cannot avoid like an unusual height or weight, a limp, deafness, blindness, paralysis, or scar. Each is as much a part of you as your momma's nose or daddy's dimple. If the feature has the potential of drawing attention away from your writing or discussion topic, get it out of the way up front. Mention it, let people know it does not bother you, and you lighten the load for them, giving them permission to look past it and focus more on your message. The comment breaks the ice so you can lead them to more important issues. Don't like talking about it? Avoid settings that bring attention to it. You call the shots and find *your* comfort level.

Tweaking Yourself

Like I said earlier, *The Shy Writer* is not here to tell you to "get over it." This book is meant to support you in your decision to deal with it. Your shyness is approachable at different levels. As the writer in question, you must decide the level of discomfort and effort you can afford in altering yourself to accommodate the change. A speech impediment can require intense attention and professional help while nervous shaking hands might only need an object to hold.

Your obligation is to name your "ills" and find the "cures." While you may possess a reserved temperament, you are not relieved of the responsibility of self-improvement. You practice your writing, your needlework, your fishing, your cooking or your makeup. You alter your hairstyle or try to lose weight. Shyness can be accommodated. Once you define your shyness factors, you need to seek solutions to those aspects that grossly interfere with your quality of life.

Will a glass of wine slow your rapid speech? How about medication for the nausea? Would note cards or an assistant overcome your forgetfulness? Pictures of an eye drawn on your papers could remind you to make eye contact.

How necessary are public appearances to your writing advancement? Do you need frequent cold calling in your schedule to make your career work successfully? A non-fiction motivational book sells well by a writer exuding a polished delivery, but a sci-fi youth novel might not need the conference tour you think it does. What public exhibitions are sorely needed and which can be substituted by behind-the-scene alternatives? We writers are a creative lot and that creativity can assist your shyness.

Writers complain incessantly about how marketing and travel interfere with their writing. A successful writer has an even bigger problem since she needs public appearances to perpetuate the success. Ever wonder when these people actually sit down at a keyboard or put a pen to paper?

It behooves you to spend serious quality time scheduling your priorities, giving careful balance to promotional efforts, the logistics of getting to those promotional events, and writing your next publication. If shyness makes those promotional efforts stressful, more time consuming, and detrimental to your writing, consider one of two things: 1) change yourself to be less shy, or 2) change your plans to accommodate the shyness. In simple terms: Fight or Flight.

Fight or Flight

In our modern world, we need to recognize that many of life's decisions are grounded in the "fight or flight" reflex. We can deal with it or we can run from it. When the boss calls us into his office with no advance warning we want to run, but we usually face the music instead. Hopefully, we do not have to fight the boss, but the act of entering his office, conversing, and concluding the situation, is "fighting." We engage in activity. Running tempts your feeling of survival when you hear "Curtis, I need to meet with you in my office, right away." But being the logical, big-brained animals that we are in the evolutionary chain, we choose to face the office meeting in lieu of hiding in the restroom. Fighting is the right decision.

When confronted with two scoundrels on the street who watch you leave the mall, do you get in their face and tell them to take a hike? Hopefully not. You make a beeline to your vehicle, jump in, lock the doors, and skedaddle away from the potential threat. We call this flight. The decision is yours. You could confront the threat. You could engage the threat. You could get your behind kicked, but instead you make the logical selection of flight in lieu of fight. Flight is the correct action.

Weigh your options. Face it or avoid it; what is good for one person is not for the other. Shyness is fight or flight. As the shy person you consider the hazard, investment, gain, and reward of your options. One person may think the gains of public speaking outweigh the fear of it. Another may feel the opposite. When all it takes to cope is a cough drop in your mouth to avoid a dry throat or a pen in your hand to stop the shakes, the balance tips in the direction of pursuing the speaking engagement. But if your neck breaks out in hives or your voice waivers till it ultimately disappears ten minutes into your presentation, it is time to decide if the appearance is worth the price to your health, your ego and maybe even your sales.

What if reality for you is somewhere in the middle? Say you attend a writer's conference in hopes of grabbing an agent's attention. Let's measure the anxiety levels at each turn. Using a scale of 1 to 5, with 1 being low stress (comfortable situation) and 5 being high stress (painful shyness), you can break down the fight or flight reflex and see where you draw the line in breaking through the shyness or planning around it.

You sign up for a writer's conference near your town. You have a manuscript completed, edited once, but not completely polished. You decided to attend because you will not have overnight expenses. A few agents will participate who represent your genre. You might have the time to completely edit the book again, but you're not sure. How do you feel?

1. No problem.
2. I'll just start and do the best I can.
3. I need to work hard on this edit.
4. I don't think I have enough time.
5. Should I even go?

The conference is in a week. You can't get the manuscript edit completed.

1. No problem.
2. Let's see how far I get.
3. Three chapters could be enough. I'll work on those.
4. Wish I'd started earlier on this. Will I look like a fool?
5. Why did I sign up? What do I do?

You arrive at the conference and recognize a few other authors. You know they have manuscripts to pitch as well.

1. Hey, girl. How are you? Bet I land a six-figure contract.
2. Yes-I'm nervous, but so is everyone else.
3. Bet her book is better than mine.
4. Hope no one wants to shake my sweaty hand.
5. Where can I hide?

You get a chance to meet your first agent. You have ten minutes to make your pitch. You did not expect the opportunity to occur when it did, but here it is.

1. You seize the day, make a pitch, and flaunt your work.
2. You apologize about the few chapters but pitch away.
3. You stumble, apologize, but proceed.
4. You talk fast, she asks you to speak up. You're scared.
5. Your sweaty hands deliver the chapters. You thank her for the time and look for a way out. You go back home and cry for missing your chance.

If you are a Level 1 writer you let life roll off your back, sometimes too easily without enough serious contemplation. For those of you at Levels 2 through 4, you have various degrees of trepidation, but you will face the music often grateful for the experience in the end. Those of you that are Level 5 writers hate to put your feelings on public display for fear of rejection, and you find approaching strangers in the form of agents, editors, and publishers deeply difficult. Your options?

*   Write for yourself and quit submitting.
*   Expose yourself to these situations more often to develop an emotional callous.
*   Find ways to approach others on your own turf where you feel more at home.

The Social Animal

Ever seen those character quizzes in newsstand magazines? The ones that ask how "social" you are like there is something wrong with not being a party animal? The participant feels like a loser if she does not crave communal activity. These quizzes list questions like:

- Do you look forward to or dread crowded parties?
- At a party do you work a room or find a corner?
- After a party do you feel exhausted or exhilarated?

Well, I'm the girl who abhors parties, wants the chair in the corner and goes home feeling like she just ran a marathon. I have never wanted to change that. I know what unnerves me and what does not. I know what settings I can function within and which ones I cannot. I understand that sacrifices are made and alternatives required when I do not follow the "norm" of social behavior. While I disagree with society's definition of "norm," I still live within those walls. But I am also one of the most confident people in the room. I know who I am.

When confronted with a public setting, I consciously weigh the need versus the want, the sacrifice versus the luxury, the requirement versus the option. When I am expected at a function and cannot justify my absence with anything other than "I don't feel like it," I attend and do the right thing. If I cannot justify attendance by an actual need like high volume sales or support for a friend or family member, I decline.

On occasion I have a grand time at public gatherings and I hate to leave, but rarely do I stay for an entire event. In my forties, I still have a negative comfort level with public appearances. I recognize the problem, do not discount it, and work to weave my personality (no, it's not a flaw) into my work with a proper balance to benefit the customers, readers, editors, publishers and myself. And I achieve this balance through self-appreciation and regular analysis of uncomfortable events. In other words, I habitually run a check of the pros and cons of my shyness versus the need for public appearance as each situation arises.

For example, a writer friend of mine has a beautiful garden book. Suzanne Pickett Martinson is young, fresh, appealing and just came off a book tour for *Outdoor Style: The Essence of Southwest Living,* Northland Press. I listened to her tales of book signing events where one person showed and others where she sold a mere half dozen copies. She did radio and television shows. She managed a baby throughout the ordeal and enjoyed the entire trek. I got tired and tense listening to her. I asked her why she attended so many appearances considering the cost per hour and the expended time, and as I launched into my spin on other options, she stopped me and said she learned so much along the way. She met wonderful people, understood how bookstores managed events and saw what captured readers' attention. She came home kinetically charged and routed that energy back into her writing, sales, and home life. Sure she got nervous, even shy when interviewed, but she quickly weighed her options and stepped forward opting for the public electricity she obviously enjoys.

You can decline events. You can attend occasions and leave early. Options – that's what this book brings to you. As a shy writer, you analyze what best works in your favor. If the stress of a book tour gives you headaches and keeps you awake at night, forego it for other promotional tactics. If you can talk yourself into public settings knowing that once you step out you do fine, your shyness is not limiting, just charming. And if you can strut out in the open and welcome the world with a big hug, that's great, too. What I hope you glean from this book is the fact that you are not a lesser person because you are not gregarious. Your shyness is an essential part of your personality. Recognize it, deal with it, and weave it into your writing world, learning to weigh when it helps, when it hurts and when there are options other than making yourself sick "getting over it."

The successfully shy don't change who they are. They change the way they think and the actions they make. There is nothing wrong with being shy. In fact, I have come to believe that what our society needs is not less shyness but a little more.

~Bernardo J. Carducci, PhD
Director, Shyness Research Institute
Indiana University Southeast

Chapter 3
Reaching Out Reaches In

- Singers
- Comedians
- Actors
- The Greater Need
- Up Front and Shy

You call yourself a shy person. I do, too. But I tell that to people and they laugh. Some people are more inhibited than others and some paint shyness a different color than others, so saying "I am shy" means different things to different people. A few paint it muted, hidden, and private, while others may give it a bright, loud coat that leads the way and rules the day, all the while masking inhibition. You can temper the colors and diminish the impact shyness has on your life, you can melt your life into your shyness, or you can find a hundred variations along the spectrum. Your comfort level determines the final hue.

Many famous people claim shyness as a perpetual obstacle in their lives. The last thing I believe I could do is to get up on a stage and become a different person in costume with spotlights shining, but that is indeed how some people deal with their shyness. As a matter of fact, that is how a lot of people deal with their shyness. They perform for others.

Performing is a rush. And we envy those that execute a stunning presentation. We credit them with natural instinct, creative genes, and extroverted personalities when actually many are reclusive, timid and bashful. Their natural instinct is to retreat, but they step up to the plate fearing the shyness more than the spotlight. Creative genes might be in their DNA strands, but so might a fear of public appearances – a possibility currently being studied by the National Institute of Mental Health (NIMH). And the extroverted personality might be a manifestation, a forced exhibition in order to earn a living and to avoid a larger fear of rejection or failure. Some call it an escape from a bashful world.

Who are these "phony" extroverts? Take a peek:

Singers

- **Ella Fitzgerald** – She recorded over 200 albums and nearly 2,000 songs working with every jazz master that lived in her time. She suffered from severe shyness and doubt about her abilities and looks, but the Depression, dire straits and a random drawing where her name was chosen out of a hat, placed her on a stage as a young teen. The American Idol symbol of the 30s, the Apollo Theatre held an occasional amateur night, and fate put Ella on stage. She tried to leave, but was told to stay and perform amid booing from an audience still hyped from the previous dance act. She learned that her home was on stage delivering enjoyment to an audience. Her shyness melted away when she released her voice, but off stage the uneasiness returned, a situation that supposedly exists to this day.

- **Donny Osmond** – Donny sought professional help when his fear of public appearances advanced into full-blown panic attacks. Imagine someone who had performed since he could walk, fearing a show in his late 30s and early 40s. He wrote his own book about it entitled *Life Is Just What You Make It*.

- **Mary Chapin Carpenter** – To this day, Mary hates the public eye. Willing to sacrifice for her love of country music, she endures appearances but fiercely fights to protect her privacy. She openly admits she loves to hide away but states that her "peace" is singing, wherever that may take her. She feels fulfilled as a singer in spite of her reclusive nature.

Comedians

- **Don Rickles** – Painfully shy, he emulated his father out of admiration. The neighborhood kidder, his father loved to poke fun at people. Don learned early that such behavior won favor and broke the ice in public settings, a way to mask his inhibited behavior.

- **Jim Carrey** – Picturing this man introverted is like finding a snowman on the beach – it just doesn't fit. Like Rickles, he soon learned that comedy melted obstacles, opened doors and made friends while helping him dodge negative remarks about his string bean thin physique and large front teeth.

- **Johnny Carson** – One sees a bit of his timidity by his calm, smooth and quiet demeanor. This man overcame his painful shyness by forgetting it on stage – a common practice by many comedians. Serving up humor to an audience gave him a personal satisfaction that overcame his natural wallflower tendencies.

Actors

- **Tom Cruise** – Mr. Confidence shows no sign of the inferiority complex he had for years. Saddled with a fear of meeting people due to frequent childhood relocations and dyslexia, he spent years hiding behind talents that did not require reading such as sports and acting. He didn't learn to overcome his fears until the 1990s and now he wholeheartedly supports literacy programs.

- **Sigourney Weaver** – Raised in an affluent family, her six-foot height, frequent moves, and mature intellect excluded her from the typical friendship circles of her peers, making books and family employees her best friends. Similar to the comedians, she learned that stepping onto a stage relieved the pressure of her shyness and opened new worlds.

- **Ingrid Bergman** – Extremely shy, she ran home from school to escape from others and threw herself into a pretend world of plays and characters she could control. Her entire life she feared the public, even cringing at the thought of restaurants, but she blossomed on a stage where she could be other people and not be responsible as herself, a common malady of actors, she once said.

- **Nicole Kidman** – This composed lady fought a stutter in her youth and to this day does not enter a restaurant or party alone.

Scientists share a reclusive nature with writers. The mere fact that they must focus and concentrate deeply on their craft makes them loners and worshipers of solitude. The world knows about the quiet personalities of scientists Albert Einstein and Thomas Edison and writers Robert Frost and Thoreau. Agatha Christie caved to her shyness and abandoned a career as a concert pianist to become one of the world's best-loved mystery novelists. When in their element, these people shine, create, and evolve. You and I understand the feeling. Unfortunately, to venture past the practice stage and into the professional world, interaction with people becomes a necessity. You have to perform in one way or another.

You need to determine where the sacrifice is made –getting in front of people or finding other avenues to sell your work without the eyeball-to-eyeball connection. Either way takes guts and innovation. Your shyness level determines the balance. As a writer, you need to get your work before the public so it can perform.

Jenna Glatzer, founder of Absolute Write, experienced years of panic attacks and still struggles with public promotion. I often wondered why such a successful person had no list of guest appearances, book signings, and conference attendances, but in researching this book I learned she is the ultimate shy writer. A self-proclaimed "former agoraphobic," she has not only successfully published several books on freelance writing, but she also contracted a book with McGraw-Hill entitled *Fear is No Longer My Reality: How I Overcame Panic and Society Anxiety and Appeared on the Bachelorette (2005)*.

I love the attitude of Christine Kling, mystery author of titles *Surface Tension* and *Cross Current*. An avid boater, she relishes quiet time on the water and at her writing. In a conversation about the fear of public performance, she mentions her concern as well as how she deals with her reservations and difficulties association with a weak, timid speaking voice. "I have concluded that this voice thing is for me like seasickness is for some others – they will never be able to conquer it by strength of mind as it is a physiological reaction. So I live with it and laugh and try to make the best of it."

The Greater Need

Many will hold onto shyness but only to a certain point – the point where they see a need greater than themselves. At this threshold, the need of the other person exceeds the wants of the self, and suddenly the shyness dissipates and an advocate steps forward. The fear of stepping forward is not in their mind at that time because their thoughts are focused upon some higher calling.

Maybe it's an instinct. I'm not a psychologist, but I do know that when a mother feels a need to protect, nurture, or support her offspring, she takes action regardless of who is watching and what other people think. Just ask any schoolteacher who has had to go up against an irate mom. Spouses come to each other's defense in a blink of an eye. Law enforcement types feel the need "to defend and protect." We have all seen a hero on the evening news step out and perform in a chivalrous manner then in an interview say, "I did what anyone else would have done in the same situation." They stepped forward in time of need.

I believe most people have an underlying need to come to the aid of their fellow human. And given a forum to do so often cuts through the fog of inhibited behavior. A few years ago, my government agency employer underwent a downsizing. As the director of administration, I held the responsibility to enact a "reduction-in-force." We had to reduce twenty people – more than 10% of our statewide workforce. Part of the process involved an educational effort to let the employees know what stood before them, what options they had, and what actions the agency had to take. Most employees feared for their careers. I had to deliver the message and ease their anxieties knowing that some would soon lose employment.

My job was secure. But I stood before two-hundred people over a three month period and explained step-by-step what they could expect, their odds, and their choices. I wrote the material and refusing to delegate such a message to a subordinate, I presented it. People asked question after question; some cried, some flashed anger, and others wore solemn masks, not knowing what emotion fit the bill. But I knew that their understanding rested upon my presentation, which had a major impact on the productivity of the entire agency. They looked to me for answers, and I told myself that I had to be their mainstay in order for them to function both personally and professionally. I amazed myself. Knowing that my words and empathy made a difference in other's lives, I unconsciously cast aside my fear of public speaking. Only after I completed the task did I realize the hurdle I'd overcome.

Your message can do the same for readers. If you feel your words make a difference and your appearance in front of a group has the potential to improve the quality of other's lives, you can drive yourself a little harder to reach out. Looking back throughout history, there are many folks who through their heartfelt convictions altered events and touched people's lives.

Many famous historic people claimed shyness as a key part of their personality including Thomas Jefferson, writer of the Declaration of Independence, who spoke in public only once at his inauguration, a public event he could not escape. He would have trouble pulling that off in today's electronically connected world. Renowned for his intellect and a visionary writer, he avoided the public eye and focused on performance behind the scenes much like the desire of many a quiet writer. But he knew the importance of his effort upon the emergence of a new country.

Einstein endured painful shyness, but he had grandiose visions of world peace. A persecuted Jew in pre-World War II Germany, he left for America and Princeton University where he became famous not only for his physics theories but also his deep emotional belief that the world had to live as one and promote a non-war environment. Wise in science and in humanity, this introverted wisp of a man stood before dignitaries, students, and political leaders to make his points, because his dreams were bigger than his discomfort.

And who remembers Eleanor Roosevelt as shy? One of my favorite people, she stepped up to the task when her husband became stricken with polio. She grew up under the firm hand of a disciplinarian grandmother and had no desire for the pageantry of politics. Suddenly her efforts meant the difference in her husband's success and continuance in politics. Causes took on new meaning and once she learned the details and depth of social ills, Eleanor grew a new earnestness and fervency for their solutions. Using her husband's name to keep him in the hearts of people and peers, she pursued answers through legislation. Her drive had a major hand in placing her husband in the White House and endearing her to the American people.

Up Front and Shy

Shyness can enhance your public image. Public individuals of few words are often noted as levelheaded souls who think on each word before deliverance making the message seem more important. Ever heard "talk is cheap?" Spoken words are simple to say and hard to take back. The shy person speaks only when necessary giving him a better chance to say the right ones. The talkative person says a lot but when do you know which words carry deeper meaning when so many are heard?

You can learn from shy people who step up to the plate. They have a mysterious quality that comes across as profound and meaningful. Funny how the reverse is true when an introvert refuses to speak. An uneducated person may see a silent bashful being as aloof, arrogant or even ignorant. As a shy person, you have a hidden strength that no one sees until you make yourself known. Admitting shyness can play in your favor.

Looking in my trusty thesaurus, I see "shy" listed as not only hidden, humble, sensitive, and timid, but also lacking, distrustful, antisocial, and suspicious. Isn't it remarkable how such a tiny word has such range of meaning? And isn't it equally fantastic that *you* determine where the final meaning lies?

Now you wonder if I am about to push you into a public-speaking class or shame you into making a television appearance. No. My promise to you in the beginning remains the same. The power is yours. The decision is yours.

Reacting with people and appealing to assemblies has to be comfortable for you to deliver your message. Dr. Phil has to appear in public to succeed. As an animal story writer, a cookbook creator, or a computer techie, you might not need to step out into the public eye. Your choice of topic, genre, subject, and message determines the demand for social interaction. And the Internet world reduces some of that obligation since you can touch so many souls with a newsletter, website and email.

I've seen people crushed with the thought of presenting to the masses – enough to alter major life decisions. These souls abandoned career dreams and discarded natural talent to avoid confronting the eyes of an audience. Intellectuals bypassed college theses, singers resigned the stage, and even teachers renounced the classroom. Then I have seen people forced to step past their horrors and then blossom as a newfound personality. Some have presented willingly and failed, and others have been pushed on stage like Ella Fitzgerald and made history.

What drives you and to what degree do you carry that drive? Only you can answer that. Define the type success you crave, then map the path to get there. And when you get there, whether you danced across conference room stages or leaped through the World Wide Web unseen, you will be right.

Let the world know you as you are, not as you think you should be, because sooner or later, if you are posing, you will forget the pose, and then where are you?

~ Fanny Brice

Chapter 4
One-on-One

- People Like Positive
- Positive Pointers
- Telephone Conversations
- Online

Most of the discussion thus far dealt with audiences, public appearances, and exhibition behavior. What about one-on-one interactions? We need to focus there since without a doubt you will face this requirement. The face-to-face dilemma cripples some shy folks as much as a stadium crowd, and you need to know how to deal with it.

A literary agent, who shall remain nameless, blogs online listing her views on writers at conferences. The number of rude and unprofessional people amazes her. She chastises them for being opinionated, brash, and demanding. The shy writer blushes just thinking about such behavior. But this same agent also complains about "babysitting" some of her clients who are afraid to speak up and make decisions. While I claim little knowledge of her field, I see her dilemma in many other professions such as the business owner and customer, the doctor and patient, the teacher and student, and the politician and constituent.

No one enjoys dealing with an overbearing ogre or a wavering weenie. Maybe I am harsh, but a description of the extremes is necessary to make the point that a middle ground is mandatory in dealing one-on-one with people. As a professional writer, you must find a comfortable middle stand somewhere along this spectrum to continue your existence.

The world is full of ideas to adapt your personality with someone else's style. And the key is simple. Treat them like you would like to be treated. Keeping that in mind along with a few tricks opens your social world.

People Like Positive

People do not look for your mistakes. They are too busy worrying about their own. Whether someone's style is muted or outgoing, his or her basic thought is number one - self. Envision a party, a room full of gals and gents, worrying about making a good impression whether it is the hair, the clothes, shoes, breath, voice, smell or conversation. Paranoia runs amuck under a cloak of smiles. Then picture yourself in their midst. As a shy person, you too think of your hair, clothes, shoes, breath, etc. STOP.

Why not refocus that energy on them? The rule here is you cannot think about yourself, and your concern cannot be your own impression. You want the other person to make a good impression instead. Speaking to everyone at the event would probably be sensory overload, so just pick five people. During the course of the evening, tell someone how you admire his smile. Tell another how you wish you had her confidence. Compliment someone's flattering color coordination and another's posture. Look for something good in each person and tell him and her in as few words as possible what that trait is. Then step back and watch.

Those five people will instantly think better of themselves as well as you, and the positive vibes you embedded into their persona will carry throughout the party. You could have three eyes and two noses, but they remember what you said. People like positive. Remember those three words. *People like positive.* I'm a nut for short astute sayings and this is an oldie-but-goodie.

The positive aspect works on you, too. In a trying situation, you tend to identify the obstacles and problems getting in your way. You personalize them. You want them to go away, and you wish things were different. You tell yourself how bad you feel and look to escape the dilemma. Gracious, what a wasted use of nervous energy! Makes me tired thinking about it.

I once had a real moron of a boss who had issues with women managers. I endured a morning staff meeting of snide remarks accompanied by rolling eyes and snickers that made me want to smack him silly. Of course, I sat amongst a dozen managers like myself, often as the solo female but usually one of two, and my hands were tied. One day in particular the remarks got under my skin; I'm not sure whether I slept badly the night before or he just caught me off-guard, I don't remember. But the result was inevitable. I left the meeting with high blood pressure, wanting to crucify him somehow in some way. Still stewing over the day's events, I ventured to the mailroom to make some copies. Another manager and close compatriot of the boss happened to need copies as well. He mentioned one of the meeting topics and I crawled down his throat with all the sharp-tongued, sarcastic barbs and arrows I could verbally sling. Embarrassed at my loss of control, disheartened at the lack of satisfaction it gave me, and angered at the man for his ability to push my buttons, I turned on my heels and walked outside to the city park and cooled off for two hours. What an erosion of self! The number of negative thoughts, actions and behaviors in that entire story are too many to count, but probably were enough to knock a few minutes off my already stress-shortened life.

So I taught myself to think positive. Move forward. Negativity is a back-up reaction where you always lose ground and face. Negative thoughts feed inhibition. Shyness in itself is not a negative, so don't read this wrong. But negativity tends to force withdrawal since nothing negative is ever comfortable. People come out of their shells when they are in comfortable surroundings. They retreat when things go sour.

As a result of this experience, staff meetings became exercises in positive thinking for me. I did my level best to turn the dark and gloomy, cold and cutting, boring and belittling into bright little glimmers of positive spirit. And when I could not participate positively, I focused on positive thoughts. I wrote down personal goals, calculated my days until retirement, wrote character analyses of people in the room and copied dialogue for use in essays and short stories. And on a particularly hard day, another lady manager and I agreed that we'd start wearing ties to the meeting to blend in better with the good old boys. We laughed at our own little secret for days, which brightened our outlook. And when things felt ugly, I took off work and wrote or gardened azaleas and petunias to clear my head. Life got sweeter. And the bad boss just about left me alone since his gestures rolled off my back. In my calming down and readjusting my outlook, I recognized the situation for what it was – the boss's own shyness and insecurity.

People like positive. Treat them like you wish to be treated. Be a mirror reflecting the image you'd like to see. And in a negative situation you can't control, treat yourself to positive vibes to manage your world.

Positive Pointers

FundsforWriters fans know I preach the positive aspect of writing, of people, of life. And in that life you have to deal with people – the good ones, bad ones, nice ones, mean ones, happy ones, sad ones, and all the ones in between. Why not be the consistent one and make everyone's life better? Here are some neat ideas to tuck in your pocket for when you are nervous, shy and forced to deal with an individual through correspondence, phone or appearance. They all work!

By far the hardest effort for a shy person is doing business with a stranger. Like the people at the party, confronting one person makes you think of your flaws and opportunity for error. Point your mind in the right direction and go armed with the positives. These pointers make the exchange a piece of cake and make the whole experience more pleasant.

- **Memorize upbeat phrases.** "People like positive" is simple and to the point. "Make this fun" is another. "I love what I do" comes in handy in an interview. When you feel negativity creeping in, inject a positive phrase to jumpstart your attitude and confidence. Make them mantras in your everyday life! Post them on note cards in your purse or pocket.

- **"He's a person just like me"** helps avoid the awestruck factor when dealing with editors, publishers, agents and seasoned writers. Awards and experience warrant appreciation, but my goodness, these people probably have indigestion and dandruff like the rest of us! And you have strengths they don't, I assure you. When you sense intimidation oozing in, remember the new millennium phrase of "shock and awe" to remind yourself that the person before you is indeed a human being who trips on the carpet just like you.

- **Practice makes good...it doesn't have to be perfect.** If you are making a pitch, have a solid synopsis in mind that you've practiced. Do not memorize it verbatim so that you run the risk of tripping up on a word and losing your thought. Just know the synopsis in general – practice it. Have it on the tip of your tongue so if your tongue gets a little tied your pitch rolls right off the end of it anyway. If you stutter, tell them you are nervous and smile. They'll probably help you along.

- **Seek the common ground.** You know those statements you seek to make your query sound personal like, "I met you at the Think Positive Writing Conference two months ago and loved your speech about queries." It's called connecting with the editor/agent. Maybe you are from the same state, love cats, or share sport interests. Savvy people dig for such tidbits to make an impression since agents and editors speak to so many people. Even if you just look the person over and tell them you have a similar sweater, seek that common ground and find a connection.

- **Hold a glass of water.** And if you are not in an appropriate setting for a glass, hold something else. Liquids help a dry tongue and the container occupies nervous hands. Bottled water is quite the trend these days and carrying it around is socially appropriate for podium speeches or small talk at parties. It steadies your hand, clears a raspy throat and give you something to do.

- **Short is good.** Short sentences, that is. If your voice waivers or the pitch changes when you are nervous, deal in short answers, sentences and questions. Your voice will have a better chance to hold steady and you do not have the opportunity to ramble in wordy prepositional phrases. Short also leads to better enunciation, while long sentences lead to slurs and more noticeable regional accents.

- **Use your acquaintance's name.** I initiate emails with the person's name, correctly spelled. It's a welcome bridge that so many unconsciously appreciate. On the phone, write the name down and remember to use it at least three times in the conversation. In person, use the name when making introductions, emphasizing points, and concluding the discussion.

- **Smile a lot.** No one can resist a smile. It sends confidence, enthusiasm, warmth, and personality. It shows your acceptance of the other person, which we all crave. On the phone, your smile can be heard, and your smile inspires positive words in your email.

- **Nod.** A slight nod of the head to another's point says that you paid attention, heard the message, and appreciated the speaker. It is unspoken confirmation and tears down walls.

- **Eye contact**. Nothing works better than eye contact, although the smile is a close second. Looking directly at someone conveys respect. You appear self-confident and attentive as a listener, and they feel assured your interest is genuine.

Telephone Conversations

A lot of the above tricks work on the phone as well, but all of this doesn't help when you are afraid to pick up the receiver. I would rather talk to someone eye to eye than speak on the phone. Why I have this aversion to phones is unknown to me, but to help I have an answering machine. In addition, caller ID tells me who is on the phone before I pick it up, and one of my ID machines even has a loud voice so I do not have to get up from my seat to read the caller ID screen. And if someone else is home, I will not answer the phone at all. Call it a mild phobia or attribute it to the shy gene in my DNA, but I do not like phones.

So when I have a telephone interview, I have to force myself to participate. In person I have the luxury of seeing eyes and sensing feedback, but on the phone I fight my feelings of negativity. Here are a few pointers I have learned over the years that could aid you in your own struggle with "telephone-itis".

- **Have a mirror handy.** If you could see the scowl on your face, you'd be appalled or tickled, but either way, seeing your reflection is instant correction. Smile at yourself and your voice will change. They are connected. I promise you cannot look at yourself and frown without laughing or changing expressions.

- **Primp.** No, they can't see you, but before an interview I comb my hair and put on lipstick. How you feel is how you talk, and personal sprucing perks you up. I even put on shoes, an extra effort for me since I work fulltime at home and adore bare feet.

- **Dress comfortably.** You want a telephone conversation to flow, and pulling at tight elastic or itchy fabric does little to aid the effort.

- **Use a long phone cord or a mobile phone**. Moving releases energy. Ever notice speakers on stage walking, pacing, waving arms, and making gestures? Part of that is getting rid of pent up nervousness. I have a quality cordless phone that I use for interviews, and I walk circles around the island in my kitchen as I talk, wave and emphasize points. Losing that energy relaxes your mind so you can think and talk more freely.

- **Cut the noise**. Make sure the kids are gone, the television is off, and the dogs are outside. Distractions kill your confidence. I schedule interviews when I am home alone. I even prefer online guest chats when the family is gone. You will learn how important this is especially during taped telephone interviews.

- **Write out your questions, answers or key points**. Phone chats require the same preparation as in-person chats. Phones, however, give you the advantage of referring to notes. If you are the caller, have bullets or even entire messages written down for reference. Writing down everything in advance imprints the words on your brain making recollection easier. Make sure your opening sentence speaks your name, business and intentions in as few words as possible. Have a pen handy to note the name you need to repeat three times, pertinent points that come up, and detailed contact information you may not already have. These lessons also work when you are the interviewee.

- **Build momentum**. Business phone conversations can bother some shy people. One way to break the ice before jumping into a necessary call is to chat with a friend first.

Get into the spirit of conversing on the phone by speaking to a familiar voice, then hang up and immediately dial the business call. Allow the momentum to flow from one call to the other.

- **Remember the water**. Make it wine if you want to, since nobody can see. Keep the whistle wet when chatting on the phone. Having the drink ready beforehand avoids the gurgling noise of pouring once you are busy.

- **Find the right person**. Ever spilled your story only to learn the other person could not help you? You feel like you wasted not only precious minutes but also that precious energy you hate to expel on a stranger anyway. Do not blow your momentum. Make sure you have connected with the proper person before starting your whole spiel.

- **Speak firmly**. They cannot see you so play a role. Pretend you are famous and confident. You will probably never meet them.

- **Dole out compliments**. People like positive, remember? A simple "You have a pleasant telephone voice" does wonders and sets a congenial atmosphere. Make sure you sound sincere. Mary Kay Ash built an incredible empire founded upon encouragement. "No matter how busy you are, you must take time to make the other person feel important."

- **Voice mail**. Leave a positive but brief message with clear contact information when you reach voice mail instead of a human being. And follow-up. Do not assume they will call back. After three voice mails, give it up. Your energy is better channeled elsewhere.

Online

Shy people can make their easiest public appearances on the Internet. One-on-one interaction takes place via email and instant messages. This keeps the other party at a long arm's length while giving you time to contemplate your questions and answers.

As a newsletter editor, occasionally I receive a complaint. I keep in mind that the complaint is for the title "editor" and not for me personally. The complainer does not know me. I always answer with an upbeat reply. One lady complained about an article I ran on Jewish writing markets and contests, claiming that I needed to address non-Jewish writers instead of favoring that one religious group. Since my FundsforWriters mission is to assist all writers, her opinion was not mine to judge. I explained that we try to reach all markets for all people as much as possible and she was welcome to offer a future submission to cover any faction she felt was overlooked. I thanked her for her feedback and said that through emails like her I learn how to keep FundsforWriters on an even keel. She remains a member to this day.

In one editorial column I mentioned how the Iraqi war overseas led to diverse opinions all over the Internet, that FundsforWriters would avoid entering the fray, and instead, would concentrate purely on the writing mission. A reader chastised me for not being a patriot and not taking a stand. In a polite, carefully worded personal reply, I informed him about my deeply rooted patriotism and how it was vested long before September 11, 2001. He did not know me well so I opened the exchange with a little history about my beliefs. I thanked him for his FundsforWriters support and hoped he understood that I could not put personal judgment about the war in a writing newsletter without it being inappropriate for some readers. The time it took for me to issue a calm and courteous response was worth the investment. He is a loyal member of FundsforWriters and sent me a copy of his new book. He offers great feedback on at least a monthly basis now. I salvaged a member and made a friend.

I hired a graphic web artist to design three ebook covers for me. With each cover I complimented her work and expressed appreciation for her prompt response and reasonable price. Flattered, she worked harder and with the final cover's delivery she included a gift certificate for a free future ebook cover.

Remember that etiquette is paramount online; these tips will assist you as you interact with all types of people.

- **Know their names**. As mentioned before, knowing a person's name and using it during the exchange shows a legitimate interest in that person's message and the person himself. We are quick to forget that emails are letters and etiquette requires a proper salutation. Do not forget your tagline and proper identification at the e-mail's conclusion – equally as proper.

- **Always respond**. As a writer you owe your readers and business acquaintances a response to an inquiry. If you intend to sell your writing, you have a responsibility to potential readers which means answering their emails. Every emailer receives an answer from FundsforWriters and when the volume exceeds my ability to answer, I'll hire someone to help with such an important task. I answer 15-year old poets and 80-year old freelancers, professional instructors and work-at-home moms, best-selling novelists and novice writers; they all receive a few moments of my attention. They express their gratitude often for my personal and prompt replies. Ignore someone and they ignore you, maybe when you need them most – when it comes time to sell your products.

- **Spell check**. How would you like a magazine interview to display half a dozen typos and grammatical mistakes in your quotes? Guaranteed embarrassment, for sure. Thousands of people will see the mistakes instead of the quality of your writing. Your poorly written email to one lone reader might wind up in dozens of other mailboxes and impact the purchasing decisions of those people, their families and their friends. Quality either leads or drags your business at all times.

- **Hit send**. Do not be afraid to query by email. In marketing a book proposal I submitted six online queries and a dozen by postal. I had the best replies via email from editors and agents. One agent converses with me to this day as well as subscribes to FundsforWriters. Another editor responded with a negative reply sprinkled with positive comments. I quickly reformatted my query asking if a deviation this way or that would be more amenable to her. She gave me great advice that led to the idea for this book. With eloquent words and professional behavior an online conversation can take a writer's career further, faster. Just remember to keep it tight, polished, and error-free.

- **People like positive**. It comes across well via Internet, too. Instead of "This article makes no sense" try "The meaning escapes me for some reason." Same message, different delivery and less adversarial. The latter is easier to swallow. Make your words positive, and you will see more doors open so people can experience whatever it is that makes you smile.

- **Remember your manners**. Offer thanks or gratitude for the other party's attention. Verbally we give quick thanks without much thought. But in writing we often omit that part. Appreciate them for reading your words. And from the other angle, thank anyone for writing to you. As often as I can, I try to thank people for supporting FundsforWriters. Manners will take you far in this world.

Speaking to an individual makes your pulse race a bit, but leads to so many opportunities. I dread a scheduled meeting with anyone. I wonder if I can match their standards for a meaningful exchange. Why I torture myself I do not know because once I start chatting, the fear dissolves and I'm eager to pick that person's mind, assist them in their writing, or learn new avenues for my own work. I pat myself on the back for weathering the ordeal and feel like a better person. But the next time I'll hesitate again and wipe sweaty palms before I start.

Individual talks are good for you professionally, emotionally, and psychologically. Humans are social animals and healthier beings from personal exchanges. Luckily you can adapt to these opportunities. Break the ice via email before chatting on the phone. Speak briefly on the phone before meeting face-to-face. Goodness knows the world has proven that online dating is a viable tool for the reclusive!

Preparation for the conversation releases pressure. Your rehearsal, training, arrangement and anticipation of a meeting might seem strenuous in the beginning, but believe me when I say the effort makes the actual experience so much easier – even downright pleasant. And your investment in another person's life builds your character, too.

I run on the road long before I dance under the lights.

~Muhammad Ali

Chapter 5
The Big Bad Throngs

- Phobia and Therapy
- Others Look Up To You
- Audience Groups
- Informal Small Groups
- Informal Large Groups
- Formal Small Groups
- Formal Large Groups

Now we address the fear that ranks number one around the world – the fear of public speaking. Anyone who does not feel a flutter or take a breath before stepping before a group, anyone who does not second guess his preparedness, or anyone who thinks public speaking is a cake walk is a rarity. Stepping before an audience takes nerve, preparation, and a firm desire to deliver a message. Sometimes the message is humorous, sometimes sympathetic, often educational, and frequently motivational, but the speaker has to believe that it is worthy in order to be truly effective.

Phobia and Therapy

A shy person hates standing before people. Increase the number of people and the fright grows exponentially. Take a

43

writer comfortable in her private study and toss her into a conference of two hundred people, and she'll lose sleep for weeks prior to the event.

Discomfort often turns into a social phobia when a shy person is faced with new settings and lots of people. Ever heard of someone tossing back a drink prior to boarding a plane? Their phobia of flying is soothed a bit by the alcohol. Some people take anti-depressants and others seek therapy to weather severe social phobia, and for many those solutions are the proper answer.

The therapy usually used falls within the realm of cognitive-behavior therapy, which involves exposing the student gradually to those things that bring discomfort, building a callous or even a comfort level with the situation. With each exposure the individual grows less sensitive. Think of it as allergy shots at incrementally larger doses until you no longer have a reaction.. The steps go into greater detail than what I mention here, but in essence the individual walks up to the fear over and over and slowly learns how to handle the situation and weather criticism or rejection, the common cause of most fear.

The method is tested, tried and true. However, how often do we as writers step in front of groups? Three or four times a year? If you have a best-selling book, your engagements number in the dozens, but the average writer still strives for that honor. And without the repeated performance, that emotional callous just does not develop very quickly, if at all. You speak once and maybe four to six months go by before you formally speak in public again. Whatever you learned from that last session might not have the residual effect preached so highly in therapy classes and you feel like you're starting all over again. The agony greets you at each event. So what do you do?

Let's say you just published your first book. Of course your publisher does not line up any events; none of them do anymore. So you are on your own, setting up book signings and offering to sell your book wherever they let you set up a table. Or maybe you self-publish and are indeed your own boss as promoter-entrepreneur. You are smack in the middle of a love-hate situation now. You need to sell the book but you do not want to deal with people, with crowds, and goodness knows, you do not want to speak to groups. Guess what? Here come phone calls asking if you would give one presentation, then another. And the bookstore wants your presence at a book signing for a Saturday literary event next month. A tug-of-war has begun between the need to sell and your need to be left alone.

The less-than-shy person is jumping up and down and whooping it up all over the neighborhood. The shy writer almost wishes she had not written the book.

FundsforWriters is over four years old. Members of the newsletters often ask when I intend to publish a book. They feel a book is the next step, and so many sweet people have told me I am ready for the task. But the darn promotional aspect of the book world held me back. The ambitious writer would call me scared or lazy. The shy writer would understand. Because with that book comes a responsibility to sell it.

Others Look Up to You

In reaching people we often have to face them. All the experts on salesmanship will tell you that a face-to-face pitch is part of a basic sales foundation. Granted we can sell our work via email and websites. We can send mass mailings and post ads. And we will sell our work a few books at a time. Slow and steady can work bringing in an income, but who does not crave the adrenaline rush of selling fifty books or signing up ten clients for copywriting services?

The personal appearance is almost a magnetic connection. The audience feels an obligation to support the speaker via the sale. It's like stopping in a fast food place during a long drive. You use the restroom but as a courtesy to the owner you purchase a cup of coffee. You do not have to but you feel it is the right thing to do. That attendee in your audience watches you go through the paces, the agony, the struggle to perform your dog-and-pony show. He wishes he could do that. He marvels at your strength. He likes your ideas and he wants to take a piece of that home with him so he buys your book, service or product.

When you speak, you are talking to people who cannot do what you do. You are special. You are unique. Others in the group have made speeches. But they can't speak on your topic, your writing, your feelings. You have a message they need to hear, and the more deeply you feel, the more motivated you become. You felt so passionate about your message that you published your words. Do you know how many people envy you for doing that? Do you know how many say they ought to write a book and never follow through?

Years ago I thought I was a mystery writer. At the time I had just pulled my writing habits out of mothballs, dusted them off and taken a course on novel writing. And I wrote that mystery novel. It took me two years of weekend and midnight writing, but I did it. Goodness gracious I was proud! I packaged that baby up in brand new manuscript boxes, sent it to a dozen agents and watched my mailbox daily for weeks.

At the same time, I learned that my mother knew Fern Michaels, the romance author, only my mother didn't realize the extent of Ms. Michael's publishing credits until I showed her. Fern was just Mary to her, a writer who loved animals and whose daughter lived across the street. Mom introduced the daughter to Southern cooking and Daddy joked with her about being a Yankee. Mom said, "We're going to a party of hers next month, you want to come? I'm sure she'd send you an invitation."

Fern/Mary turned out to be a beautiful person who loved people and any excuse to get a group together. Nervous, and of course, shy, I enjoyed the party with my parents and husband and spoke to Mary briefly. She knew I was writing a book and offered to read it and make any introductions necessary. Such an opportunity! Such a lesson! A few weeks later, I dropped the manuscript in the mail. Mary made good on her offer. I received a brief written critique, and she asked an agent friend to look it over.

Wondering why you don't see "mystery author" in my email tagline? Because Mary (and her agent) promptly and politely let me know that the work was rough and without the edge it needed for traditional publishing. But what she added to that review was worth my computer's weight in gold. She said to count my blessings and remember that my family was my first priority to enjoy here and now. She said she knew and envied my family, and I should be proud of my life with or without a novel. The novel would happen if it was meant to be, and family time should not be sacrificed for a book. She also said I deserved to be proud that I had completed a novel because so few people do. She forwarded a signed copy of her book *Celebrations* with the words "One day I'm sure you'll sign one of yours for me. Enjoy, Fern Michaels." Rejections do not get any better than that.

I felt immediately indoctrinated into a cadre of people known as authors. And that is exactly how your audience wants to feel. They do not belong to that fraternity, and they affiliate the word "author" or "expert" or "consultant" with success they wish they had. Look at yourself as their mentor. Give them a moment or two of enjoyment and exposure to the world you teach and write about. Talk to them. Make them feel better. When they do, you will, too.

Audience Groups

Still petrified? Then let's dissect audiences into types, see where your comfort zone is, and define what you prefer to remain off-limits. As I repeat throughout this book – you choose when to be shy and when to step out, and no one can define your comfort level but you.

I place audience groups into four categories: informal small groups, informal large groups, formal small groups and formal large groups. You will feel at ease or distraught in different degrees based upon the type of audience, but by understanding the dynamics of each one, you overcome many hurtles and learn how to adapt.

I like informal groups of any kind. For some reason I do not feel quite as exposed if the group is in a circle, impromptu at a restaurant, or seated around a group of tables in a coffee shop. My writer's group in Phoenix meets at a Borders, usually seated in classroom style in front of the chairman or guest speaker.

That's bordering on the formal side of things in my book, but the nature of the people makes it informal.

However, one month the group asked me to talk about grants. A higher power must have been looking out for me because our usual more formal location in the store was occupied that day, so the bookstore manager moved us to the children's section. Here we were seated in tiers, on carpeted primary colored seats amidst bunnies and balls. My tension level dropped fifty percent! Sitting with one leg tucked up under the other, I felt like I was talking to girlfriends.

At a conference you have little or no choice – the setting is formal, the agenda is structured and the people are seated to accommodate the numbers of attendees instead of to promote interaction. As the guest speaker you might want to come prepared with suggestions on the room arrangement. If you have the opportunity, do what you can to adjust the environment to your need.

Let's look at each of these groups and make some suggestions on how to approach a presentation for each.

Informal Small Groups

Informal groups have characteristics and opportunities that are clearly identified. These groups are casual, natural, everyday, and ordinary, usually fewer than two dozen people. Those work for my style! Just dressing me up in a suit and heels raises my blood pressure. And natural means you will likely feel comfortable in your surroundings. If the number is small, you have the potential for an easy and fun event.

Still queasy? Informal groups also mean that your talk can be informal. You control whether you do a reading, tell stories, answer questions or involve the group. The smaller the group, the less I speak because I like questions and answers. A small group is more inclined to ask questions. So I schedule my talk for half the time period allotted, and before I know it the time is up. Answering questions feels like a chat to me. I try to use people's names in a small group setting because usually they all know each other or at least wear nametags. It brings us closer and makes them more accepting of me. When I am the only person talking, I feel alone and on stage.

For some writers the small informal group is too unstructured, leaving them more in charge and the group more expectant – too much pressure. These folks prefer distance. They like a podium as a protective buffer.

You might feel that the small, informal group is too close for comfort and chatter opens up too much discussion, too much exposure. Maybe you do not like to shoot from the hip and field questions. Talking the whole time gives somewhat of a protective zone between you and the crowd. You talk, they listen, you sit down. Structure your speech as you would an essay with a thesis, supporting points, summation and repeat of the thesis giving yourself a conclusive ending. Give your talk a final "amen" flavor and the group won't feel compelled to ask questions. Avoid insulting the group, though, and at least stick around afterwards to talk one-on-one.

Small and informal lends itself to eye contact. Smaller groups also pay more attention. You can see them better and they know it. Just think of your high school and college days. The amphitheater Psychology 101 classes had a hundred people in them. You could read *Cosmopolitan* and get away with it. But a senior level class might have a dozen attendees where the teacher knew when you took notes or doodled. The small group feels like it is performing, too, so it is a two-way street. You are safer using people's names in this setting, and you have less chance of humiliating someone. But if you see someone hesitant to make eye contact, do not call attention to him. You understand their fear.

What about the small informal group where you are not giving a speech? Do you like the feel of a social rather than a lecture? Have a party or drop-in instead. You make your presence known with an opening thank-you-for-coming, chitchat with everyone, and close with another thank-you-for-coming. Have someone else do the thank-you speech and just mention you are present, if you prefer. Have fun with a creative theme for the event, and practically hide behind the motif with the attention on a bigger picture than you.

By now you are picturing yourself in this size group and analyzing where you stand. If this feels right or less awkward for you, include only small informal groups in your marketing plan as a writer. Plan to speak only to a dozen people and schedule a larger number of appearances if this is your niche. Or only schedule little parties with finger foods and small talk. Keep yourself comfortable so you can focus on the matter at hand – your writing and your expertise. You speak easier when your shoulders are not scrunched up under your ears and your hands are not sweating.

Informal Large Groups

Let's focus on the informal but expand the group to more than 25 people. In my mind I envision retreats, book fairs and some conferences in this category. Book fairs may have a speaker talking to a hundred folks while three hundred more mill around the booths. People around the fringes of your audience stand up and sit down randomly. Such appearances lend themselves toward humor and one short story after another.

Not long ago I wandered through a book fair seeking mysteries and taking notes about marketing when my husband spotted a security detail. You have to understand my husband. A twenty-six year veteran of federal law enforcement, he lives cop stuff. We recite security rules under my roof like you teach children table manners. Sandra Day O'Connor was guest speaker at the book fair and had local police and federal service types surrounding her as she browsed the booths. Ten minutes later she stood at an outdoor podium and spoke about the importance of books and history. I stood in the back under a tree since the chairs were taken, and watched how she handled the crowd. She told tales of her grandparents and parents in the Old West. She told story after story about cattle rustlers, cow-pokes, drunks and lawmen. The setting was informal. Some attendees wandered around the edges of the group. She did not answer questions and the air was relaxed and unceremonious. She controlled the presentation without being stiff and official.

A large informal group can be the best of both worlds. You reach a lot more people but with a casual style which makes you more comfortable. Lots of writers like speaking in such a setting. You might still need to take questions, but not many because the size of the venue inhibits everyone's hearing. A little squeaky voice from the fifteenth row might not be heard at the front or at the back. The speaker repeats the question, answers it and moves on. You can lose an audience that way, especially if the room is informal without decent acoustics, as was Justice O'Connor's setting outside under an outdoor canopy.

A lesson here is simple but often forgotten. Know the venue where you will speak and design your speech around it. If you have handouts but the group is irregularly seated, expect major disruption when some people get skipped. If you have an overhead presentation, will the corner seats or front and back rows see clearly? If you want the attendees to actively participate with each other, will tables be in the way? And, of course, know if you will speak with or without a microphone. If you are provided a mike, what kind will it be, stationary or wireless? Handheld or lavaliere?

I move around a bit when I speak, plus I'm a klutz. Put a cord in my way and I'll trip on it every time. Give me a microphone to hold and I'll wave it around like a magic wand or hit myself in the teeth. If I had a PowerPoint presentation I'd probably tap into some Internet porn site instead of my slides. I keep it simple and avoid complications. The "extras" make me more nervous.

You might be a master at stage tricks with technology that give you grand pizzazz. I know people scared to speak without a gimmick because it gives them confidence. In their minds the toys, bells and whistles not only help tell a good story but also buffer them from being stared at by an audience.

Formal Small Groups

I used to affiliate formal with pantyhose. Thank goodness business suits and classy clothes come with pants. Formal small groups basically are informal small groups with polish and structure. There is a courtly decorum affiliated with the talk.

Small formal talks are great for educational or business topics. You are making a well-defined presentation. I did these in my previous life as a federal government director when the boss and his lieutenants needed a briefing. I also taught business classes to as few as four people. This type of speaking ranks highest on my emotional discomfort meter.

In this setting, the goal is to speak to impress not entertain, and some speakers attempt to undermine the formality with humor, ending up appearing silly, nervous and unprofessional. Ever seen someone laugh before a group and the group remain silent? Tears your heart out, doesn't it? When you have a solemn function, treat it with the dignity it deserves. Come fully prepared, be punctual and strictly adhere to the agenda and timeframe.

A formal group is a tough audience in any circumstance, especially if others in the group have to present, too. To make it easier on yourself, remember that they are nervous for you, just like you are nervous for them. No one likes to watch a failing speaker. Empathy is a big-time emotion in a group setting, so when you step before those eyes, realize that they hope you do well. When you stumble, physically or verbally, they are holding their collective breath praying you regain your footing and move forward. When you perform successfully, watch the smiles and relief on their faces and the nods of their heads. Few people enjoy making a formal presentation, but weathering one sure gives you a heightened sense of personal satisfaction.

Formal Large Groups

You might think this is the iceberg of all public forums – the formal humongous group. "Large" doesn't do it justice. Standing on that podium before a couple hundred or more people, you feel like you are about to get married. The sheer formality of the event focuses hundreds of pairs of eyes on you.

Imagine tuxedoed and sequined bodies seated at round white-skirted tables adorned with dessert dishes and carnation centerpieces. The irregular clinks of coffee cups on saucers and restrained coughs do nothing but remind you that everyone is listening. You pray that Captain Kirk of Star Trek fame will somehow make time pass in a nanosecond and transport you back to your own table – better yet, at home in your recliner. The room has so many people expecting so much!

You know what? In this social setting, these people are dying to be entertained. Quite the opposite of the small group, this setting has more latitude and opportunity for a charismatic presentation – a talk with personality. Do the sheer numbers scare you to death? Water down their effect. Pick a table and talk to just those people seated there. Staring at a sea of heads has a way of tongue-tying the best of speakers, but selecting someone to directly address mutes the immense nature of it all.

Have your notes and your important thoughts bulleted for reference. With each one, select a new table. Aim your words at that individual and complete the sentence. Move on to your next bullet point and speak to another person. The thought of all those eyes on me used to turn my stomach into knots until I forced myself to gaze right back. Connect with one person at a time. Ask them to listen to you because you want them to learn. Offer your phrases to them like a dose of friendly advice to a best friend. Wrap them with your message and feel good doing it. These are people who need you and you want to help! Reach out, enable them, and empower them with words they can take home and use.

Poof. You're done.

I'm serious! Getting personal with your speech is uplifting – for you and the audience. Time speeds by, leaving you breathless in the end. Your information must be genuine to you to pull this off, but if you are confident about your message, this isolation exercise works well.

Frankly, the informal groups comprise most of your public demands as a writer unless you reach the famous author ranks. Informal groups are easier and more fun, if you can make the leap to call public appearances fun. Consider size and design strategies to create a situation more to your liking. Tossing out all speaking engagements might ease the pressure now, but someday someone is going to make demands on you to smile before a group of fans. As a matter of fact, if your writing takes off like you want it to, your fans will make even greater demands on you. Even if you limit yourself to drop-in parties, show yourself to the world. Out of sight, out of mind is a tried and true cliché. Assure readers you do exist and do have a message to deliver. As a writer you want your words to have a lasting impression.

Show class, have pride, and display character.
If you do, winning takes care of itself.

~Bear Bryant

Chapter 6
Honing the Skills and Confidence

- Book Signings
- Simple Social Settings
- Personal Obstacle-Busters
- Mantras

Before you run for the hills screaming, "I can't do this!" let's learn more tricks, habits and exercises that help you work through those intimidating faces we call...customers.

In this chapter, I will give you settings and a list of tools to take with you. Armed with mechanisms to confront people and events, you can stand a little taller. These will give you something to think about other than your discomfort level. You can make it a game!

Book Signings

I hate these things! I would rather speak to a room full of suits than hang around a table with a smile that hurts my jaws for three hours. Read writers' postings online and find hundreds of authors who live for book signings. They feel rejuvenated when someone asks for their autograph. I would rather face a beating.

So I've researched other writers, watched actual signings and tallied some pointers for you. Here are ideas that can help, so start taking notes.

- **Stand up for yourself.** No, don't pick a fight. Literally stand up. Sitting puts you in the position of being looked down upon which subconsciously gives you a feeling of subordination. On your feet, you feel stronger, speak more easily, and project stronger vibrations. Professional coaches tell students to stand if at all possible to not only look more positive but feel more confident.

- **Move around and dispel the energy.** Who says you have to stand behind that skirted table all dolled up with no place to go? Grab a few books and walk around the store if the fans are not lined up at your table. Hopefully you have a nametag that says "Author" on it. Walk up to people in your book section and shake their hand. Do not force yourself on them. Ask if they read your type of book and either engage them in small talk, if they are so inclined, or leave them alone if they are not. Respecting them often leads to a book purchase. At least hand them a bookmark as you walk away so they will remember what to purchase later.

- **Have your essential statements memorized.** Every public relations type harps about you having a brief synopsis of your work ready in case you are asked. You know, like those famous sound bytes out there in commercial media land. Create two or three that roll off your tongue instantly when you are asked:

  1. **Who you are.** (Hi - I'm Hope Clark, founder of FundsforWriters and author of *The Shy Writer*.)

  2. **About your book.** (*The Shy Writer* helps writers understand their shyness and work through it to better promote their careers.)

3. **If applicable, what your company does.** (FundsforWriters is a website company that provides writers with newsletters and books about grants, markets, and good business practices.)

- **Prepare Q & A's.** Brainstorm questions that customers may shoot your way and prepare some safe answers. Write them down so they are embedded in your memory. You know the ones – why do you write, how did you start writing, how did you get a book published, why did you write this book, where do you get your ideas, how long have you been writing, how do I get to be a writer, who's your favorite author, what's your favorite book. Practice and preparation makes you more at ease so you do not have to ad lib.

- **Find a partner.** Ever thought about sharing your book signing with another author? With three or four or more? Do you know that as an "author" you have an intimidation factor? In the customer's mind you are practically famous and some readers are afraid to confront you seated there in your suit, scarf and heels. But, put a panel of authors together and it becomes a party. A cadre of authors will have at least one extrovert in the lot who will draw attention and, as a shy writer you could use a partner with a little noise and flair. Let the extrovert draw the customers while you smile and look approachable, and you both sell your books.

- **Bring an assistant.** Another alternative to the author partner is the assistant. No one has to know the assistant is your spouse, niece, neighbor or best friend. Find someone who is outgoing, give her a nametag of "Author's Assistant," put a book in her hand, and turn her loose. She walks the room, store or mall and draws the customers. She leads them to your table where you busily write, sign or do something that looks official. After making introductions and handing the customer a book to review, she dismisses herself and seeks more prey. The concept is that you appear a bit important and the customer feels special. And if you picked the right personality for the assistant, she is having a ball.

- **Fairs and conferences.** If the solo nature of bookstore signings keeps you up at night, channel your efforts toward conferences, book fairs, retreats and workshops so that you dilute the focus on you. As one of dozens, you feel like a team player instead of a lone ranger.

- **Skip them.** If they irritate you that much, skip the book signings altogether. Instead of this arduous event eroding hours of time, set up meetings at a bookstore where you drop in, sign books and move on. (Don't forget your autographed-by-author stickers for the book covers.) Scheduling is still necessary to ensure the store has the books, but imagine the potential sales. Take a list of the bookstores in your community, call or email each one and introduce yourself by offering to drop by in a couple of weeks to sign whatever books are there. To avoid embarrassment, most bookstore managers go ahead and order the books when they otherwise might not do so. If you arrive and they do not have a supply of your books, pull them out of your hat – in other words, bring them with you just in case. Ever prepared, you happen to have ten copies for the unprepared storeowner.

Simple Social Settings

Parties, writers conventions, garden clubs, chamber lunches, weddings, wherever you have a chance to say you are a writer, you can expect questions and chatter about what you publish and why you do it. As you may already know, word-of-mouth is powerful communication. If someone feels charmed after meeting you, expect ten more people to think you are the best author in the world. But, snub or ignore someone and suddenly you are not worth two cents, and twenty of their friends will dislike you even though they have never met you. Talk is cheap but it can be expensive, too. You are "on" as a writer at all times.

I once had coffee in a local bookstore with a writing friend. We had just come from a poorly organized presentation that people literally walked away from. We discussed the shortcomings of the presenter in a setting we thought was private. Unknowingly, at a neighboring table a woman overheard our opinion. Two weeks later the woman wrote me about a writing question and mentioned the negative conversation between these "two ladies" and how she felt sorry for whoever was being talked about. She did not realize I was one of those ladies. I knew it was me once she identified the coffee shop and approximate date. Amazed that fate brought us together, I identified myself as the probable culprit and attempted to make amends. I silently chastised myself the entire evening. You never know who hears you in public, so keep your words and deeds clean and your negative opinions confined to very private gatherings. Eating crow is not fun and will not help sell your writing. Remember that your email and your conversations are all on public display.

Are you more scared than ever? Don't be. Keep these pointers in mind:

- **Smile.** Others will talk about their novel, their thoughts about a novel, their uncle's novel, or some story that ought to be made into a novel. Smiling lets them know you are listening. We all want others to care about us. We need to feel loved. Plus, your smile takes the place of a thousand words and makes the other person do more of the talking.

- **Listen.** Don't just nod like a bobble-head. Listen and make an occasional comment that shows you heard. Regardless of the caliber of the content, give the person a thumbs up or word of positive friendly advice. Making someone else happy will do two things: make them talk more so you talk less, and make them think you are a caring human being. A win-win scenario for sure.

- **Watch how others work the room.** Every group has a charismatic person. Watch what he does when he greets people and see how people respond. While you are in this public forum, use the time to learn from those socially comfortable. Listen for chit-chat ice-breakers and see how folks respond to different situations.

- **Let others start the conversation.** Scared to walk up to people? Let them walk up to you and initiate contact. Shy people shrink away from opening a dialogue. But when someone approaches you, be polite and respond showing gratitude that they spoke to you.

- **Prepare some topics.** Practice your small talk. List topics in which you excel. Study current events. Read some recent book reviews. Having subjects readily available gives you a savvy appearance. After all, who intellectually prepares for a party, dinner or conference anymore? You do, of course. Your self-confidence rises when you come prepared. You not only will impress but you also will feel more comfortable.

- **Stand.** Feel stronger on your feet, looking people in the eye. You have more flexibility in your movements, and that ability gives you a chance to expel pent up energy that comes with nerves. I often speak with my hands, which is mighty hard to do behind a table or from a chair.

- **Learn the name**. Speaking to a stranger is awkward. Ask the person's name and use it three times in the conversation. Personal barriers fall and people's ears perk up when they hear their name. They feel special if the tone is positive and defensive if the words are negative. Using someone's name in a positive light encourages the connection and raises their personal opinion of you.

- **People love positive**. Now where have you heard that? I said it before and I say it again. Positive breeds positive. Instead of, "You don't make any sense" say, "I struggle with that point." Sound awkward? It takes practice. Get into the habit and dodge the negatives in your conversation at all times. The day of the party or conference gives you little time to develop a routine of no-negative, all-positive thinking.

Personal Obstacle-Busters

Want ideas to take with you in any situation? Try these suggestions. Pick one or two and work at them. Practicing all of them can overwhelm you or defeat your purpose. Weight management gurus say losing pounds and inches is a change of lifestyle – one step at a time. Going cold turkey from pizza, beer and midnight banana splits will drive you up the wall and lead to diet failure. But limiting yourself to cheese pizza, diet cola and frozen yogurt the first month can ease you into the proper mode.

- **Take a class**. While Toastmasters is a common and still marvelous suggestion for public speaking phobias, taking any class has a similar effect. Some of us have not attended school in years, even decades. Sitting amid students warms you up to public settings. You learn to join in conversations and contribute in a social environment.

- **Dry off sweaty hands**. If you worry about your hands being clammy and damp, wear clothes with loose pockets. When you see someone approach, nonchalantly stick your hand in your pocket and dry it off on a handkerchief, tissue or the cloth itself.

- **Carry a drink.** Remember the water trick in an earlier chapter? In social settings most people have a drink.

Sipping on one alcoholic beverage all night not only wets my whistle but also soothes my nerves. And the moisture on my throat makes my voice steady. Any type liquid will serve the purpose.

- **Deep breaths.** You may think it's only a psychological tool to take deep breaths, but it is also a physiological exercise. The added oxygen stimulates your brain and slows your blood pressure. It also flows over your vocal cords warming them and regulating a voice that might be a little squeaky from fear of use. Deep breathing clears your head and settles you down from head to toe.

- **Shaky hands.** Hold something like a drink, a pen, a book, business cards, or a purse.

- **The bathroom break.** Know the bathroom location and if feeling stressed, visit it to breathe and calm down with cool water. Smile at yourself in the mirror. I like to put on a new coat of lipstick.

- **De-stress.** After a function I feel drained and run for the bed or recliner. Others may need a different release. Vocalizing a really big scream is a true exercise in stress relief. Please do this outside of a conference or social function, maybe in your car with the windows rolled up or you will certainly face questions about your sanity.

- **Find a mentor.** Locating a confidante who can talk or walk you through social interaction works quite well. Finding a seasoned public speaker mentor can tear down emotional walls for you and build confidence. Having your mentor in the audience might be the ticket to help you perform admirably. Mentors are marvelous tools in all avenues of life. Mentoring and being mentored gives you a satisfying glow.

- **Join a group**. Find a writers group, church group, educational group, theatre group, any kind of group with committees. Your writing group might host an annual conference. Your church group might sponsor a Thanksgiving charity dinner. Your theater group should have a play coming up, and an educational group might feature children's presentations. Sign up for one of the committees. The interaction is practice in people skills. No one says you have to lead it or even hold a key position. Just be a player.

- **Hire a partner in crime**. Find a speaker who covers a similar subject to your writing. Give him a percentage of your proceeds and ask him to incorporate your work in his presentation. Sit in the back of the room, bow when introduced, and voila! You have made a public appearance.

- **Sit on a panel**. Can't face the room alone? Agree to panels or group arrangements. Conferences love using panels of authors, publishers, editors and agents. Receive the publicity with a fraction of the spotlight. Panels are a lot easier than standing isolated and alone on stage.

- **Request a podium**. That box of wood or little metal stand somehow empowers you. A podium might not be much between you the "them" but it might be enough to relieve some jitters, allow room to spread your notes, and provide a mental buffer zone.

- **Phone callers**. Scared to call the radio station, book store manager or gift shop owner? Get your "assistant" to do it for you. Consider her your own public relations assistant. Just make sure this special person knows your work and can reliably schedule and coordinate.

- **Phone call pitches**. So you have no assistant. Write down your points in advance, ask for the right person, give your brief, well-designed pitch and make a specific request. "Could you stock five copies of my book? May I schedule a book signing in September?" More about this later.

- **Tell people you are nervous**. When you verbally stumble, laugh it off and tell people you are jittery. They will commend you for facing them in spite of your shyness, and you will no longer be hiding your fear. Cindy Daniel, author of *Death Warmed Over*, Quiet Storm Publishing, says, "I'm always very nervous to speak in public. My husband says it never shows – but I usually end up coughing and getting a dry throat so I have to pop a cough drop. I always explain to the audience I know it's rude to have something in my mouth and offer them one, too." When she lacks a cough drop, she sips a cola and murmurs, "Hmmm...Jack Daniels." Now that's an ice-breaker for both the speaker and the audience.

- **Blushing**. You get embarrassed, blush, then blush that you blushed. Relax. Drop your shoulders and release your muscles all over. Let that belly flop, too. Stick it out. It makes you feel looser. Admit you blush! When it happens, own up to it, and it passes more quickly. Even consider mentioning the tendency to your audience. "There I go blushing again!" It makes you one of the common folk and moves you off that pedestal.

Mantras

I like this section. Here is where you tell yourself that you are indeed a superb human being for being a writer. When you need some assurance, put these little phrases in your mind and recite them.

- **People like positive**. Did you think I would let an opportunity slide by to repeat this, did you? The public adores positive people.

- **They want me to succeed**. Everyone loves a winner! Those people want you to do well.

- **I've come a long way**. Give yourself a pat on the back.

- **I am a writer**. Why do writers doubt who they are? Do actors have to own an Oscar to be classified as real actors? Break out of that pack and own up to what you are.

- **I can help**. Everyone loves to come to the aid of others. Helping others is a natural human instinct. Your writing, your appearance, your words are gifts to others' lives.

- **It's good to be me**. Self-explanatory. Revel in yourself.

All our lives we are preparing to be something or somebody, even if we don't know it.

~*Katherine Anne Porter*

Chapter 7
Shy But Sharp

- The Niche
- The Plan
- Your Customer Personified
- Pointers
- Shy But Sharp Promotion

This chapter brings out your strengths. You are smart, bright, creative but just shy. All those shining things that make for successful people are yours. And being the quiet person you are, you tend to be introspective which means you'll think a little harder about what you do before doing it.

What did we do a dozen years ago when the Internet was not in everyone's house? Younger writers probably do not remember what it was like, but I can still feel the zing when I first saw my screen connect to some intangible entity called the Internet. I joined AOL at a time when it was version 1.5 or something – that was in 1992. The world opened up to me and I spent hours reading, just reading. I am a research sponge and could not get enough of it. Then I learned email. How cool! Spam was not an issue and ten emails was a busy day.

Today the Internet is a networking and commerce necessity. Anyone without it is left at a disadvantage and that includes writers, especially writers. Those in the business of words, stories, reading and journalism have to be savvy navigating the

Web. Your readers might not all be computer literate, but the stores, distributors, newspapers and reviewers sure are, and they sell your writing wares. Part of your job is to be popular online.

First, get a website. I started my love of the web with a personal web address http://www.chopeclark.com. Later, once I established FundsforWriters, I added web pages to that personal site. The first *Writer's Digest* award that I won for 101 Best Websites for Writers applied to that original FFW website http://www.chopeclark.com/fundsforwriters.htm. In hindsight it wasn't such a bad idea. I threw my own name and the company's name out there in one fell swoop. I spent days looking for the most relaxing waterfalls, greenery and flora to decorate my site and demonstrate that this was my alternate world away from the federal government day job that zapped my energies. In those days of dial-up the site took forever to load, and I learned to improvise with smaller pictures and elementary designs.

Each website grew simpler as I became more frustrated with those choked with blinking ads, scrolling shouts, and tiny advertising fonts. Today's site delivers the message with ease without clutter and distraction. Take a peek, if you have a minute, and check out http://www.fundsforwriters.com. As you can tell, I evolved to two websites. FundsforWriters grew over the years to the point I needed clearer identification and more space. You can find my third domain at http://www.theshywriter.com.

The Niche

With the quick distribution and ease of online information, you have a simple path for success. You have no excuse not to specialize and become known for some thing, some niche, some genre, or some idea. I discuss gimmicks in another chapter, but here you learn about becoming an expert on some concept in this immense world of unending thoughts and ideas.

What do you write? If you have to stop and think about it, you are not niched. Writing about everything and anything does not garner you the respect you deserve – or the fans needed to sell your work. Everyone has a niche. It can be as defined as pets, babies, weddings, or World War II battleships. Or it can be as open as family life, business, history or travel. You can be a romance novelist or a biographer. You can write for all young people or simply grades K-6. When someone thinks of you, they must think of what you do at the same time. Your name, slogan, logo or book title pops right into their head if you plan it right.

Look at all you have written. What is the underlying thread that ties most of the pieces together? Can't see it? Then pick out your best works and connect the dots. There it is - your little piece of the writing world. What you write best and most often characterizes your niche. Write down in ten words or less what you do. Pick good tight words and create a clear message. As we discussed in a previous chapter, create essential statements to have handy in a public setting. Say who you are – short and sweet.

The Plan

Now comes the part that grew from my experience in business. Planning. Now that you put a name to your specialty, where do you want to go with it? Answer these questions:

1. Where do I want to be at the end of one year?
2. Where do I want to be at the end of two years?
3. Where do I want to be at the end of three years?
4. How much income do I need for the first year, second year, and third year?
5. Where will that income come from?
6. For the first year, what are my planned quarterly writing accomplishments?
7. For the first year, what are my planned quarterly marketing accomplishments?
8. For the first year, what are my planned quarterly sales accomplishments?
9. For the first year, what are my planned quarterly expense expectations?

10. Who is my customer base?

Groan and moan all you want to, but the successful writers do some, if not all, of the above. You do not have to take the financial details down to nickels and dimes, but you need a map to your destination. Dislike the business stuff? Then write for self-satisfaction; there is nothing wrong with that. Do not expect to sell your work for very much or very often and do not whine when the income falls short of your expectations. When you write, you are a writer. When you sell, you are a businessperson. If you do not like the business aspect, then write for your own enjoyment.

Shyness is not a limiting factor when it comes to planning. But as a shy writer, you have to work harder to grab a share of the market that outgoing writers naturally snatch. At a book fair you compete with that charismatic chatterbox in the booth next to you, but because you have a marketing plan, you placed coupons in the fair's program that is handed out at the gate. Your coupon entitles customers to a free gift at your booth and you place a sign for obvious display at your booth repeating the coupon offer. There are ways, my friend, to compete. But sitting there watching the charismatic chatterbox attract the majority of the customers is not the time to brainstorm. Planning begins ahead of time.

FundsforWriters receives lots of email about dreams, wishes and goals from writers. All look forward to their names in print. But earning a living from the effort is not about the writing, it is about the selling. Authors attribute their lack of sales to every reason in the world except a lack of marketing focus on their part. They write well, publish a nice book and speak in the area bookstores. So does every other writer. Or they submit article after article to *Field and Stream, Family Circle, The Smithsonian,* and *Seventeen* but do not understand why they receive rejection after rejection. Or they send pieces to small publications that pay five cents per word and fuss about the low income.

Strategic planning works for any endeavor. You establish the big goals, then back up and set benchmarks or stepping-stones to reach those goals. Say you want to write a mystery novel and earn your living as a mystery writer. You have bills to pay and lots of obstacles without a plan to overcome them. So come up with a plan. Just remember that these scenarios are fabricated. You create your own projections based upon your family, living standard, time expenditure, and dreams. You may freelance part-time because you like the day job, but plan like a full-time writer to capitalize on your energy investment. Make the most of your talent.

1. Where do I want to be at the end of one year?

Have a mystery written and in the editing stages. Have half the bills paid off to prepare for future of writing fulltime. Still working the day job.

2. Where do I want to be at the end of two years?

Have the book under contract and another mystery at least half written. Have three-quarters of the bills paid off to prepare for writing fulltime. Have X number of dollars in the bank for emergencies.

3. Where do I want to be at the end of three years?

Have the first book on bookshelves, the second under contract, and the third started. Have the bills paid except for the mortgage and have X number of dollars in the bank for emergencies. Quit the day job and write fulltime. Find affordable health insurance before quitting.

4. How much income do I need for the first year, second year, and third year?

1st Year:_____
2nd Year:_____
3rd Year:_____

Insert your comfort level here. Could be $10,000, could be $100,000. Allow for inflation and consider reducing it if you pay off major bills.

5. Where will that income come from?

1st Year: Something other than writing, that's for sure.
2nd Year: Something other than writing, except for maybe the advance on your book, if you are extremely lucky or wonderfully talented.
3rd Year: Writing, hopefully, with a back-up plan, just in case. This tells you that you need to rely upon anti-writing income (funny how that's the way we see it). And it means you do not quit work to write until your first book is contracted and selling, and you know you can write another book. Otherwise, count yourself broke unless you have support from a spouse, inheritance, or an inside tip on a horse at the track.

6. For the first year, what are my planned quarterly writing accomplishments?

Write a third of the book for three quarters. Edit in the fourth.

7. For the first year, what are my planned quarterly marketing accomplishments?

Second quarter, shop for potential agents and publishers.
Third quarter, send queries with first three chapters polished.
Fourth quarter, send more queries since the first set didn't pan out. (Hopefully not the case.)

8. For the first year, what are my planned quarterly sales accomplishments?

None in the first year. Even though the answer is "none" you want to write it down so that this question is a habit for subsequent years. Answer these questions like you would those on your income tax – a deadline you cannot forget.

9. For the first year, what are my planned quarterly expense expectations?

List your living expenses and writing expenses. Cut back on living expenses where you can realistically. If you fully intend to make an income from writing within three years, go ahead and count your career on your taxes as "writer." If you do not have an income (i.e., profit) by the end of the third year, you are a hobby writer according to the Internal Revenue Service and are not entitled to deduct your expenses. Make sure you understand the rules of each.

10. Who is my customer base?

Mystery readers? Not specific enough. What are the age range, gender, income level, and geographic concentrations of your reading base? Once you acquire an agent, some of this is done for you, but you cannot land an agent or a publisher without defining your customers because they are part of your book proposal.

We answered these questions for the novel writer. What about the freelance article writer? The income starts right away in the first year and the marketing is different.

1. Where do I want to be at the end of one year?

Writing 20 hours per week and earning a quarter of my income from writing. Pay off a third of the bills and set up a savings account. (Have measurable goals for specific bills, not general ideas.) No new debt.

2. Where do I want to be at the end of two years?

Writing 30 hours per week and earning half of my income from writing. Pay off three-quarters of the bills and put X number of dollars in savings. (You worked smarter and found editors that continue to like your work.)

3. Where do I want to be at the end of three years?

Writing 40 hours per week and earning all income from writing. Have all bills paid off, six months worth of expenses in savings for emergencies, and affordable health insurance.

4. How much income do I need for the first year, second year, and third year?

You decide but remember as you pay off bills you need less income unless you put the difference in savings. Try hard not to spend it. Define each year based on the bills paid off, savings going in the bank, and growing needs of your family. Save as if your life depended upon it.

5. Where will that income come from?

Define the dollars you expect each year from writing, the anti-writing job and the other family incomes. Interpret it into dollars for each year.

6. For the first year, what are my planned quarterly writing accomplishments?

1st and 2nd Quarters:

Keep thirteen queries in play at all times. Sell ten percent of them. Submit half to markets paying over $50 and half to markets paying under $50. See what I mean by specifics? Define your own but make them measurable and accountable.

3rd and 4th Quarters:

Keep thirteen queries in play. Sell twenty percent of them. Continue the 50/50 above and below the $50 line (or other parameter).

7. For the first year, what are my planned quarterly marketing accomplishments?

First quarter:

Open a website that clearly explains my niche, strengths, history, and resume. Order business cards. Study professional writer groups for membership and rewards.

Second quarter:

Start a monthly newsletter through a newsletter service like Yahoogroups, MSN or other avenue. Update website as articles are sold, posting your clips online as part of your resume.

Third quarter:

Swap ads with similar publications to promote your work, and seek a new market each week. Continue to update the website.

Fourth quarter:

Purchase an ad in a publication that does not swap ads and watch for feedback on your investment.

8. For the first year, what are my planned quarterly sales accomplishments?

For each quarter, list income and numbers of sales planned. At the end of each quarter, compare what you actually sold to your initial projections.

9. For the first year, what are my planned quarterly expense expectations?

You have writing expenses and family living expenses. Knowing your cash flow tells you quarter by quarter if you are on schedule or behind schedule in your goals. If you set unrealistic goals, adjust them each quarter. If you reached some goals ahead of schedule, adjust accordingly as well. Remember you will have ups and downs on this wild writing ride.

10.Who is my customer base?

Moms? Women? Guys? What are the age range, gender, and geographic concentrations of your reading base? What are their occupations, entertainment preferences, and income ranges? As a freelance writer, you sell articles to magazines, but it's the correct composition of readers that determines your sales and popularity with the publications. Know who reads your stuff. Putting it on paper and defining your stereotypical reader hones your focus for future articles.

Your Customer Personified

Most writers do not personify the typical reader who buys their words. The intelligent writer can envision the generic customer. When you write a novel you analyze the protagonist, the antagonist and secondary characters in great detail. You even have a notebook that lists their likes, dislikes, hangouts, hobbies, quirks, strengths, weaknesses, eye color and genealogy. While you hope your customers cover such a wide range that you cannot possibly identify hair color, you can identify a swath of the population who qualify as your readers. Analyze them. Become intimately familiar with them. Write for them in not only your work but in your promotional efforts as well.

Walking through the mall, look for your customers amongst the crowd. Go to places you think they would go. Market yourself where these souls gather. Stop and think, "Who reads my work?" And then work hard to embrace their needs. Thinking in this manner puts you in the proper mindset to better sell yourself. If your typical customer would not routinely go in a bookstore, then do not go there. If they prefer quiet locales, place your work in their path. If they read certain publications, have your services conveniently listed in those pages. If they like fried chicken and potato salad, find a way to put your name and product on a counter or on a placemat under the plate. Subtly be where they are and intrigue them with your writing. That is the way to sell writing.

Pointers

So you feel better about your niche. You write business articles for 25-40 year old college graduates in the $50-80,000 range. Or you write young adult ethnic stories for ages 10-16. Maybe you prefer short story collections for families with children still at home or humor stories for adults approaching retirement. You are creating form, shape and definition to your focus. If you have not done it already, tweak your mission statement about yourself to make it ring true.

Let's hone that identity with some pointers on reaching your niche. Spread that persona far and wide without stress.

- **Set up a website AND keep it current**. People get annoyed with aged material and it hurts your credibility.

- **Create a following**. Offer a newsletter that caters to your niche and demonstrate that remarkable expertise you have.

- **Join clubs, groups and professional organizations** for writers, co-members of the niche and seekers of the niche. Memberships not only spreads the word about you but also keep you abreast of new information. You must stay current!

- **Publish an ebook.** Do you know how easy these books are? Purchase ebook software, use Adobe, seek a publisher, or simply prepare it in Word and password protect it. For publicity, give them away. For money, sell them on your website. The name and title page should refer to you clearly and brightly. Create an affiliate program so others can sell your work for a commission.

- **Write articles about your niche**. Sure you write novels, but you can write articles about writing your novels to help spread the word about how great you know your niche-stuff within your novels. Thousands of newsletters and websites crave 500-1000 word pieces that any writer can pen in his sleep.

- **Email tags**. Shame on you if your email does not have an automatic signature that tells people who you are, where to find you, and what you do. My kids in college get jokes emailed from their mom with that tag along the bottom. They might forward the jokes to a potential customer.

- **Give advice**. Write a column and publish yourself in a newsletter or generate it for another editor. Give brief, sound advice to those interested in your niche. FundsforWriters originated because I could not keep up with the emails asking for financial answers. Consider syndication if your customer base is in need of constant updated information and you have time to write regularly and can keep tight deadlines.

- **Swap ads**. Whether on a website or in a newsletter, ask to swap information with like-minded souls. FundsforWriters swaps ads with writing-related sites, newsletters and entrepreneurs. Swaps save funds and reach potential customers. Be prepared to swap text copy as well as online banners ads. I like the 120 x 120 pixel box ads that fit down the left-hand side under my menu. Moira Allen's website Writing-World (http://www.writing-world.com), does a crisp clean job of presenting this type of ad. Remain true to your niche or you risk diluting it.

Advertising where your customer base is the minority, or accepting ads for non-niche topics confuses Internet surfers who read quickly then click past your site.

- **Teach a class**. People love learning, especially when they are fresh to the niche and excited about the future. Create an autoresponder class by taking an aspect of your niche and reducing it to six lessons. An autoresponder emails these to the student on a weekly, biweekly, or whatever basis without you writing individual emails. You choose whether or not to include homework and interaction with you. The more you actively participate, however, the more you charge for the course. Search the Internet for "autoresponder" and find all the information you need. They are quite simple to use.

- **Chat.** Some online chats drag out forever, but some of the good ones offer fabulous information and networking. Chats can be habitual so control yourself. You learn current tidbits of good information from the movers and shakers in your niche. Whether as a guest or a participant, you can spread the word about yourself in a good chat room. I participated as a guest for Fear of Writing, http://www.fearofwriting.com, and had a ball! I offered advice and gained new FundsforWriters members who probably spread the word about FFW in other chats and forums. Love that word-of-mouth! You find free chat-hosting sites all over the Web.

- **Sponsorship.** Support a writing contest. Or assist a public event at the library, the Chamber of Commerce, or the YWCA. Judge a contest, give a donation, or offer free advertising on your site. Affiliate your name with another event and splash it to a new audience. WebMomz, http://www.webmomz.com, sponsored a grant for entrepreneurial moms starting a new business. As a supporter of business sense for writers, and with so many of my members being moms, I connected those dots and offered sponsorship. The FundsforWriters logo sat on that website in plain view for months for a sponsorship fee much cheaper than advertising.

- **Mentor.** Giving back to others is a social responsibility. As the opportunity arises, reach back and help someone who struggles as you once did. You should never arrive at the point you are not reachable. Not only is mentoring the right thing to do, but you gain an ally, supporter and fan who will spread the word about you to others.

Shy But Sharp Promotion

While you create those short-term and long-term plans for your writing, incorporate the shyness factor in the benchmarks. What are your parameters? You will not speak before organized groups, but you will do book signings. Maybe you appear in public only five times a year. You prefer local appearances and refuse to travel outside the state. Your limitations are yours to plan around. Identify them, face them, and weave them in your plans.

You might consider trying a speaking engagement and then judge how you feel. When talking about your specialty or the book you gave birth to, a fire may light up inside you that overcomes and consumes some of the shyness factor. When I speak about FundsforWriters, or the simple options open to writers who cannot find work, I get excited. At the risk of sounding cliché-ish, the proper term is "passion." Passion cures a lot of ills and makes life happier, livelier, and meaningful. Speaking might serve a worthwhile purpose in the right setting under the right circumstances.

Once you define where, what, when and how you deal with people, particularly your potential customers, orchestrate avenues to make sales and promote your work. Become savvy and sharp when it comes to balancing your emotional security and your marketing. Be shy and still sell yourself.

- **Print.** Expect to have more written promotional material on hand when you do not speak. Call it compromise or a necessary expense, but when oral words cannot sing your praises, let printed ones do it for you. More on this later.

- **Conferences and conventions.** Send door prizes, posters, coupons, and free samples to as many conferences as you can. Make them unique and outstanding in the midst of the mundane so prevalent at these events.

- **Smart selection.** Why send advertising of your mystery novel to a writer's conference? Why have a children's book sales booth at a writer's conference? Unless you are selling a writing product (like FundsforWriters), you do not try to sell to other writers. If you write science fiction, find gatherings of sci-fi fans not other sci-fi writers. Send coupons for your book to those who read it, not those who copy it. Sure we are like souls, but we are not normally each other's customers. That sci-fi author will make more sales from coupons placed in comic book stores than at writer conferences. Know your customer base and stick to it.

- **Book clubs and reading groups.** Send a free autographed copy of your work to established writing groups. Then offer a discount to the members if they select your book for discussion. Find out when they plan to discuss your book, and offer discussion topics. Send thank-you notes, preferably in longhand, and on stationery depicting your book, logo, or pen name. Make these people true-blue fans and each will tell ten other people about you.

- **Order forms.** Put order forms on your website, in your books, on the back of postcards, on fliers, even on bookmarks and business cards. Make a purchase so simple a customer places an order before he has a chance to think twice. Leave nothing to the imagination because in that fleeting moment a person strives to figure the how, when, or where of ordering, you lose him.

- **Business to business.** So you wrote a business or self-help guide. Thought about advertising in the break rooms and cafeterias of businesses? Make a sale in those places, and the word spreads like wildfire. Talk to management and offer employees a discount. Better yet, talk to management and offer a discount if they order fifty copies to pass out to employees. Even better, ask management to order a hundred for customers as piggyback deals to other purchases. Offer to autograph them and you might cinch a cool deal.

- **Charities.** Offer similar discounts to charities as you would to a for-profit business. A $100 donation to the charity could result in them signing a deal with you and sending donors each a free copy of your book for a like donation. Donors are customers to charities. Charities need promotional tools to encourage donations. Do you have an anthology that fits the theme of a shelter, literacy group, or youth-at-risk nonprofit? Police hand out teddy bears to kids in trouble in many cities thanks to partnerships and grants with people like you. A children's book just might work a similar magic, plus you might find a grant to compensate your arrangement with an LEA (Law Enforcement Agency). Your writing aids their mission and they help your sales. Consider charities and the donors as potential players in your customer base.

- **Schools.** If you write for children, schools should be your best friends. States have grants for writers who partner the education process. Grants can pay for a few hours or a few weeks of your assistance and expertise. Go to the National Endowment for the Arts (http://www.nea.gov) or the National Assembly of State Arts Agencies website (http://www.nasaa-arts.org) to find your area or regional representative. Connect through school principals and teachers as well. They know lots of grant doors to open for visiting experts like you. Talking to kids is pure fun unlike the conferences and book signings you abhor. Who knows? You might talk a school into purchasing your book for a hundred students.

- **Catalogs.** Approach catalogs that sell items related to the world you write in. Gardening catalogs, children's catalogs, clothing, sports, fashion, home decorating, self-help, stationery, or wildlife catalogs might like to list your publication amidst its pages. Before you toss those junk mail catalogs, flip through them and see if your publication fits. Some people cannot stand to put down a catalog without ordering something. And spontaneous or compulsive buyers live for those catalogs, especially around holidays.

- **Video.** Do not like public presentations? Film yourself in private. Give a short talk, pitch your book, or thank a group for allowing your work to be displayed - all on tape. Personally invite them to your website. I am amazed that more conferences or more authors do not utilize this tool.

- **Your cover.** Make that book spine one that captures a roving eye canvassing the bookshelf. When all the spines in your genre tend to be dark, make yours jump out with a pastel or white cover. If the covers of your competition have block lettering, make yours script. Create a metallic cover, an embossed cover, any kind of cover that does not look like the competition. Go to the bookstore and you instantly grab ideas. It is not enough to have a nice cover. It has to be nicer than the neighbors on the shelf.

- **Be prepared.** Wherever you announce your work, offer to supply the easel, the poster, the display, and handout material. Make the task easy for the party accepting your work. Make that business owner happy to do business with you because you go the extra mile making his job easier.

- **Press.** Whatever you do, broadcast an advance, accomplishment, or business deal with the press. Whatever ground you break, sing it to the media. Play up the local papers especially. Everyone loves hometown celebrities. See Chapter 9 for press releases.

Most people do not plan. Others start a plan and put it on the shelf. You know better than that. And the few writers remaining do not pursue these creative tactics, so now you have the competitive advantage. You make money doing what you love because you know how to put a name on it and go after it...with a plan.

Shyness can be an integral part of your plan, as long as you make arrangements accordingly. You think outside the box and color outside the lines to promote yourself, your writing, and your image. Yes, you are shy. But defining your niche and planning your future makes you wise.

Ninety-nine percent of failures come from people
who have the habit of making excuses.

~George Washington Carver

Chapter 8
Gimmick the Name of the Game

- What's In a Name?
- Setting and Characterization
- The Gimmick of Location
- I Don't Have a Book
- Fun Stuff

Gotta get a gimmick! Heard that before? Gimmicks forge a lot of sales in all arenas. Gimmicks for logos, slogans, colors, designs, mascots and methods often lead a product to success. You want your name to be known, but since you are on the shy side of the personality fence, you hesitate to jump out there and grab a microphone. Why not create a gimmick that does it for you?

Start with yours truly. C. Hope Clark may be known in a few circles, but FundsforWriters is known in many more. The name came so naturally to me because writers kept contacting me about how to find money for their bills, writing and promotional efforts. Writers always need money. I learned quickly that the Internet harbored a zillion sites leading with the word "writer." So I discarded that as the first word in my search for a title. I worked in the government lending and grant world at the time, and "funds" was the common name for money. Our very existence depended upon the funding of Congress, the amount of funding allocations, the repayment of loan funds, and the approval of grant funds. I think of "funds" instead of "money." So when the name rolled off my tongue so easily, I knew I had a winner.

After four years of FundsforWriters (one word because I couldn't figure out how to separate the words in a tagline in FrontPage), I figured it was time for a logo. Oh, I had a makeshift one I did online with a free font program, but I did not have the proper files to create banners, stationary and the like. So I contacted Business Polish in Phoenix and those two ladies treated me like gold. And here we are today. Green and black for money and class, and a logo that sweeps like a dollar sign at the front and a writer's flare at the end. I feel really bonded to that logo now, especially since green has always been my favorite color. It's me! Now, I shoot the FundsforWriters name all over the place in ads, bylines, sponsorships, and articles.

What's in a Name?

Gimmicks are a must today. You may not want a business name, but you need identification, a well hammered thought, or keenly designed concept that precedes you and your work. When people think of it, they think of *you* and smile. Let's look at some fine examples:

- **Chicken Soup for the ...Soul.** A magnificent identifier developed by Jack Canfield and Mark Victor Hansen. A soother for the soul, whether you are talking about moms, gardeners, golfers, teens, or pet owners. And everyone wants to be in these books because the public adores the series. *Chicken Soup* personifies quality, heartwarming stories.

- **The Publishing Game.** Fern Reiss's name may not be as well known as her logo, but her business is growing in leaps and bounds especially considering she is a self-published author. Her logo is a chess piece being moved on a board, and each new title has that image in a different color. Selling them in a box set is so enticing. I ordered it in the blink of an eye.

- **Sue Grafton.** As a mystery fan I adore Ms. Grafton's books. I have her complete set to date all lined up across my shelf – *A is for Alibi* all the way to *R is for Ricochet* – and I'm always watching for the next letter as soon as it comes out. Even if you forget her name, you remember the alphabet murder mysteries or Kinsey Millhone name.

- **Deborah Donnelly.** Each one of her books centers around weddings and a murder mystery. And each cover has a bride on it – *May the Best Man Die, Died to Match*, and *Veiled Threats*. Very catchy.

- **Diane Mott Davidson.** This author serves up culinary mysteries. Each one talks about food, chefs, caterers and gourmet cooks. With names like *Prime Cut, The Grilling Season, Dying for Chocolate, Sticks and Scones*, and *Chopping Spree,* you get hungry in the bookstore.

- **Anne Rice.** Talk about horror! This woman has the whole "vampire and the damned" concept neatly wrapped up and her fan club and sales attest to the theme and its appeal. Ever heard of *Interview with the Vampire*? This movie was based on her book series.

Are you hanging out there in the freelance world looking for a place to land, only to take off again, floating aimlessly looking for another place to momentarily plant your byline? If you like to write lots of things, how are people to recognize you? How will they find your work? The old "a Jack of all trades is a master of none" saying applies here.

One day I may write mysteries, but right now I have to follow the natural flow and energy that is FundsforWriters. When I decide to write those novels, I will use a different name to differentiate myself, the way Nora Roberts uses J. D. Robb, because C. Hope Clark is so closely linked to funds, advice and the motivational fun of FFW.

I do not write cookbooks (a personal enjoyment), gardening books (always a joy), or how to raise teens books (my mentoring sideline) without diluting what I built with FundsforWriters. FFW takes a lot of effort for me to stay on top of the latest in grants, competitions, and markets. To do the work justice, I must dedicate my time and my attention to the subject. Writing about many different topics makes your career confusing to your readers and you lose that powerful niche identification.

With the planning tools in the previous chapter, you can put a finite point on your goals and the steps you need to reach them. Having goals helps define your gimmick. Consider the following; the nature of your writing determines your choices.

- **Pen name.** My name is Cynthia Hope Beales Clark. Do you know how many Cindy Clarks are out there? Literally thousands. So I chose my favorite name, Hope. It is less common and seems to fit the FFW mission.

- **Business name.** Make the name attention grabbing. A business entitled "A Good Job" could be a landscaper, printer, florist or carpenter and sure won't capture someone flipping quickly through the yellow pages. But "A Good Word" narrows the search to someone in the literary world, making it easier for customers to find you.

- **Series name.** Diane Mott Davidson calls her books the Culinary Mysteries. And who does not know the Harry Potter series, the Jack Ryan series, or the James Bond series? Your character, geography, or nature of your writing can give you an identification. The *Cup of Comfort* series just beckons, don't you think?

Setting and Characterization

Use setting and characterization in your promotion. I use money in my book fair and promotional venues, but only in a subtle and tasteful way. I do not want to be confused with get-rich-quick schemes of other vendors. I wish to lead with help and motivation, not cash. At my booth you first notice my logo, then the color green and then you might see a good luck coin, bubble gum silver dollar or bookmark with a dollar bill emblem on the back. "Freelance Hope" is engraved on my nameplate pin.

Cynthia Brian is a Renaissance woman with such titles as wife, mother, actor, model, success coach, interior designer, gardener, artist, casting director, writer, best selling author, producer, world traveler, furniture designer, television and radio host. She is head of Starstyle Productions® and founder of the nonprofit Be the Star You Are®. You will not see her without a star of some sort. Her office is upholstered and adorned in stars. She wears star jewelry and even sports a star wand to bestow confidence and empowerment to her audiences. The author of *The Business of Show Business*, *Be the Star You Are*, and co-author of *Chicken Soup for the Gardener's Soul*, she is often called the Star Lady. Coupling the star image with a brilliant smile, she reaches out and uplifts people.

What is the color of your writing world? When you go in public, do you have a motif that precedes you and speaks loudly on your behalf? As a quiet writer not fond of public forums, you need setting and characterization more than ever. Watch someone with a sharpened image (i.e. gimmick) and see how people react. They assimilate it with success, which interprets into sales because the whole package sends a message. And the theme becomes instant shyness protection.

When I venture out to a conference, I wear the FundsforWriters colors- green and black. I chose the colors in the logo to represent money and printing ink, but when I transferred the colors into my apparel, it hit a home run. I forgot green was one of my best colors, and black just speaks classy, so with my black slacks and bright green blouse, I greet writers next to my matching banner. Works like a charm (and makes me look skinnier).

Think public relations. Think sales. Envision a book fair. You have two writers side by side. Both have their books on display. Both have attractive covers and striking titles. But one sells more books than the other and this is how it's done.

- **Dress for success**. She dresses like the best-selling author she wants to be. Dressing comfy and cozy makes you feel a little better at the end of the day, but does not register with the crowd. The author that appears dignified and classy says she means business and probably wrote her book the same way – with style and quality. She smiles and appears to be enjoying herself even if the panty hose are hot. And her nametag says AUTHOR in bold clear letters.

- **What is this book about?** Ever attend a book festival and notice all the booths look alike? Ever visited a booth and picked up the book to determine its subject? Whether you use posters, banners, or lapel buttons, broadcast your book's meaning. Do not make a reader wonder what genre you write. Grab the mystery reader with a big Who Dunnit sign so that twenty feet away he knows to rush over and purchase a copy.

- **Professional promo.** When you develop a logo, business card or banner, make it professional. Construction paper and magic marker banners spell "amateur" and may chase away a lot of sales. Better to spend the money up front and create a polished appearance that attracts customers than to save money but compromise your image. A cheap banner normally means a cheap book to the average reader. I spent $199 for a logo and it's been worth every penny down to having it developed in all the right formats – jpg, gif, eps, pdf and bmp. It saved me $39 at the sign store when I handed them the eps format that kept them from creating my image from scratch. That logo is worth every penny.

- **Adorn with gimmicks.** Are you a cookbook author? Where are the free food samples and recipes? (Be sure to check out local health regulations regarding serving food.) Are kitchen aprons and gadgets decorating your space? Is your table covered in a checked tablecloth and an apron wrapped around your waist? Or maybe you write romantic fiction. Decorate with items from the settings in your stories – New Orleans, Tucson, New York or LA. Is your story Victorian? Have a ball with the beads, lace and tatted tea-colored tablecloth with roses in an antique bowl. Flaunt the fancy! Garnish with gimmicks. Drape western blankets, greenery, bolas, oriental lanterns or ABC streamers around the booth to set the stage for your book and identify its theme.

- **Plenty of information**. Selling time is not the time to be frugal. Have tons of business cards, order blanks, postcards and bookmarks. Do not ration. It looks amateurish. Display your information in a durable display or in such a fashion that the goods do not fall apart, blow away, or dent easily. And if you unexpectedly run out of books (such a good problem), have order forms and offer discounts for the reader's inconvenience. A potential buyer's judgment of you hinges upon a good, initial impression with superb customer service.

- **Theme**. If the exhibition you are at has a theme, incorporate it into your display. If it does not, make sure your own display theme is clear and eye-catching.

- **Pictures**. Use posters and pictures, not just words. Your book contains the words you want the public to read. Hang posters of your book and photos of you signing books. (This also helps them identify you.) Use headshots and casual candids. Display your prizes, awards and commendations. The more you show them, the less you have to say as a shy person hesitant to strike up a conversation. Raise the awareness and identification of your work with non-verbal displays.

- **Coupons, gifts, and package deals**. Ribbons, bows, and cellophane catch a shopper's attention. Some writers package symbolic items with their books in gift baskets around holiday time and capture sales. And coupons or discounts make almost anyone stop and take notice. I offer writing conferences a free TOTAL FundsforWriters newsletter subscription as a raffle prize and $2 coupons for the goodie bags. Many writers decide to purchase a subscription after getting that little $2 card in their hands. The equivalent cost of a soda and a candy bar makes the difference in whether or not a sale occurs. And do not forget to offer deals. Package two of your own books or partner with another author. Offer your book to gift shops, clubs, and businesses as a sales extra with their merchandise. Think creative enterprising. Everyone loves a good deal.

When you write, you are a writer. When you sell, you are a businessperson. I once left a book fair very disappointed without a book in my hand. The fair was an annual event in a pretty large city with dignified speakers, but the booths had the image of a county fair. I wanted a good mystery, darn it, and I could not find one. One booth had a banner proclaiming, "Best-Selling Mystery Author;" it was the only booth that clearly noted the genre of the book being sold. And when I approached other booths in hopes of finding a mystery, someone jumped on me to tell me how their book was written, why it was written, and where it was written. I quit approaching booths for fear of being hit with a sales pitch. Remember, I'm not one for public appearances, and if you jump me when I pick up a book, you scare me off.

Later, I spoke to a friend who had a booth there. She published a beautiful book and since it involved the paranormal, she had a crystal ball, greenery and other decorative paraphernalia at her booth. I knew the gist of the story, but a casual observer visiting her booth could not tell if the book was supernatural, mystery, nonfiction or romance without reading the book jacket. I told her that authors forget that a reader wants to enjoy the story and judge for herself if it's good or bad and only after the reader accepts the book as a good read does she want to know anything about the author. She immediately altered her banner for future events and clearly addressed what her book was about – a paranormal mystery.

The Gimmick of Location

Where you flaunt your work makes a difference. The motto "location, location, location" is not limited to real estate sales. The local dress shop might prove to be a lucrative market for romance stories or fashion sense advice but a bummer for science fiction or sports. Marry the potential sales of your writing with locations and think wisely doing so.

- **Theater.** Ask to do book signings or hand out material at a theater when a showing resembles your work. Do you write comedy? Consider a display when a blockbuster humor flick is scheduled. At a multi-plex where anything is shown at anytime, you can pitch your latest release and hand out first chapter samples, bookmarks, coupons, or postcards. The more fun the handout, the better. And remember that people will have their hands full with greasy popcorn, so make it something they can easily tuck in a purse or pocket. Harlan Coban published mini-books of teaser chapters and had them distributed at theaters.

- **Long lines.** Ever watched how impatient people become while standing in long lines? If you are daring enough, or if you can grab your extrovert representative, consider handing out material and offer signed book sales where people must wait to enter or participate in a function.

People are more prone to listen since they are bored with the wait. Vendors sell water, balloons, programs, hats and toys to those same people. Give them a quality souvenir to take home in the form of your book.

- **Restaurants.** I know a South Carolina author who writes mysteries. She signed her third release on several occasions in the restaurant she mentioned in her story. Everyone loved it and sales were great.

- **Featured site.** Just like the author above, consider attendance at a locale mentioned in your work. While you write, consider using a unique but accessible location so that you can capitalize on the press later. The featured place can be a bench in a park like *Forrest Gump* (quite famous now in Savannah), a ballpark, a café, or a simple pastry shop. And where possible, leave a display of signed books on consignment with the manager.

- **City, community, county, or region.** Some writers specialize in regions. You can think of them in a snap. Patricia Cornwell uses Richmond, Virginia. Kathryn Wall uses Hilton Head, South Carolina. Stephen King places stories in Maine. Ask the appropriate Chamber of Commerce to display your work in their lobby and place fliers in their new resident and new business brochures.

You can take any story you have written and insert usable and location gimmicks. If you are a commercial writer, consider the clients you already have and use their location. As a children's writer, you can appear at puppet theaters, PTA meetings, children's pizza party restaurants, or little league ball games. Envision your name and book title on the back of an entire soccer team's jerseys for a season. Romance writers can attend bridal showers and lingerie shows or partner with someone who sells the merchandise. How fun! These venues are much more fun and less intense than a solo book signing, not to mention more productive.

I Don't Have a Book

Sooner or later a writer wants to write a book. The need seems to be in the blood. We all think that publishing a book is the pinnacle of success. In the meantime, you write articles, short stories, essays and news features and do not have a book. How does a gimmick work at this level?

Simple ideas might be the logo on your website, the jokes in your articles, or the pet parakeet referenced in all your columns. You write animal features and partner with shelters and societies that protect wildlife and pets. You author government exposés and understand the bureaucratic circles of Washington, so you hand out American flag lapel pins. Maybe you have a reputation for tear-jerker short stories and offer initialed handkerchiefs for sale on your website.

Some gimmicks send a subtle yet empowering message. Who you regularly work for often makes an impacting statement. "Debra Johnson with the Washington Post" says a lot. Educational credentials such as MFA or PhD assist your credibility without speaking. If professionalism and prompt performance come to mind when your name is spoken, you have a powerful gimmick. These habits can do nothing but enhance your career and open doors. Do you have these qualities to add to your repertoire of gimmicks?

- **Organization.** Your records are straight, your facts confirmed, your copy legible, and your invoices prompt. When you say something is done, it is. If you say it is accurate, it is. You do not realize how precious reliability is to an editor, agent, business owner or entrepreneur. When your name means "organized," they love to see you coming. Just ask Julie Hood, founder of The Organized Writer, http://organizedwriter.com.

- **Promptness.** Editors adore you because your assignments come in under the deadline. And if editors love you, you have it made as a freelancer. You land choice assignments and regular offers. Impress several of these editors and you have a career as a contributing writer.

- **Empathy.** The readers of your articles feel you understand their needs. Empathy is a wonderful trait to have because it keeps readers coming back for more of your care and understanding.

- **Humor.** It never fails you and your readers thrive on it. Just ask Dave Barry. The world craves laughter.

- **Consistency.** Whatever you do, you do it like clockwork. If you publish newsletters, they go out on time. If you write articles, they make a worthy point. When weaving short stories, you amaze the reader. And you do it all the time, without fail. Become known for the consistency of your work. It's a kissin' cousin to reliability.

Fun Stuff

Freebies are the gimmicks of commerce. Give something away and you draw a crowd. Remove the writer's hat, don the vendor's cap, and look for giveaways that match the flavor of your writing world.

- **Pens.** All over the Internet you can find commercially engraved pens for 25-50 cents each. Buy in bulk and they cost less. This is one of the few publicity gimmicks you can justify purchasing at the economy level. I know one writer who has pens and postcards that go with her mystery novel. She autographs the book then encloses the pen with the book and a postcard saying that the book was signed with that exact pen. How cool is that? Romance authors often sign with feathered pens.

- **Bookmarks.** While postcards are good for signing notifications and package deals, bookmarks are reusable.

Use postcards for mailings or gift sets, but for handouts, bookmarks are your best bet. Put ordering information, website information, or services offered along with all contact information on the back after you put an impressive image on the front. I collect bookmarks and like to rotate using them in my novel of the week.

- **Food and candy.** I use candy coins with foil covers. They catch your eye heaped up in an oversized brandy snifter on a green tablecloth. Green and white mints work, too. Something about free, pretty, and unusual finger food grabs attention. Individual wrapping is a must, though, for health reasons.

- **Contests.** At the Time Warner BookMark website, http://www.twbookmark.com, you find oodles of contests by all their authors. They publish a newsletter that lists all the new books and contests that include such names as James Patterson and Michael Connelly. Sponsoring a contest is a good attraction. Join with other authors and sponsor packages of like books or same genre publications. Include coffee cups, subscriptions, bubble bath or fishing lures with the books and you have a tempting offer. These make good door prizes at conferences or for gift sets. Just make sure your name or logo is in plain view, large and legible.

- **Holidays.** Poetry for Valentine's Day and children's stories for Christmas never fail. Become known for writing seasonal work. Some writers love the opportunity to write about Easter dresses, Thanksgiving meals, Hanukah celebrations, back to school lists, prom night warnings, Memorial Day remembrances, and New Year's resolutions. You could be the seasonal scribe. Partner a release with a community celebration. Do not forget festivals, fairs and fiestas. Maybe FundsforWriters and April 15? Maybe not.

- **Automobile Advertising**. Your car and the cars of your friends and relatives go to school, work, the grocery store, and the doctor's office. They roam the interstate highway system and the entire country if you count vacations. What does your personalized license tag say? Don't have one? Design one that talks about writing or your work. Everyone reads personalized tags. Can't fit a suitable name on your tag? Then use bumper stickers. Give them out during the holidays and coax your family into displaying them on their cars. Worried about sticker glue on your car? Then create magnets. I once saw a contractor who converted his business cards into magnets, stuck them all over his car, and had "take a magnet" lettering on his windows. Everyone that drove by that vehicle strained to read the magnets. And you could tell by the gaps in the neat rows that some interested people had helped themselves.

- **Cards and Stationery.** Take a step further. Order Christmas cards imprinted with your logo or Santa holding a copy of your book. Incorporate your logo or book title into everyday note cards and thank-you notes. Buy sticky notes prepared with your website URL. Every time you write an editor, publisher, printer, or businessperson, use logo stationery. Drop business cards in all your mail. Order postage stamps with your book cover, author picture, website or logo at http://www.photo.stamps.com. Publicize your writing image every chance you get.

- **Unique.** I once saw a posh purse/luggage store offering custom designs on quality leather bags! Instead of pictures of the cocker spaniel that they recommended, use your book cover, your logo, or your name and website. Wherever you can put your name, do it but only with style and taste or risk hurting your carefully cultivated image. Better to do a few quality items than too many cheap ones.

- **Jewelry.** I have seen mystery writers adorned with pins that represented their suspense tales. Their book cover was designed with little charms dangling that represented various clues and key items from the storyline. I can find "hope" jewelry all over the stores these days. If you write history or romance, consider vintage jewelry. Maybe your story's locale is in New Orleans where you can find Mardi-Gras brooches. Animal lovers have a slew of choices as do sports and outdoors writers. Promotional stores can create enamel pins in any shape, color, and size for you and your fans to wear.

- **CDs.** One romance author had a title song written for her romance story by a close friend, then she offered it as a package deal with the book. Wise woman! Michael Connelly had a jazz CD prepared with tunes that represented his book's setting. He also had a DVD prepared with interview, readings, and artistic views of the Los Angeles geography described in his book *Blue Neon Night.* Or go audio with your book. CDs cost pennies and recording devices fit your computer for $300. Be careful not to record anything for which you do not have permission or copyright ownership.

Make the gimmick game a fun one, and go a little overboard to pack a punch with the public. You know how silly commercials can be – bordering on the ridiculous. But the carefully chosen ridiculous theme sells and makes your marketing life as a shy writer so much easier. Go totally ridiculous and offer full case purchase discounts of your book. Splash these "special book offers" all over the paper and Internet or channel mailings to signature businesses where this little gimmick might land you a hundred-book sale in the snap of a finger!

The writer wants to leave a scratch on the wall of oblivion saying, "Kilroy was here."
                                                    ~William Faulkner

Chapter 9
The Press and Media

- Press Releases
- Promo Kit
- Interviews
- The Interviewer in You

Want to freak ninety percent of the population? Tell them to stand before a television camera. They squeal, shake, exclaim and jump around. Or they freeze and reply with eyebrow gestures because their vocal cords shut down. You'd think that stepping in front of actual bodies would upset people more than the media, but the concept of appearing before millions makes a difference to many.

The media can make your career. Newspaper, television, radio and Internet coverage spread the word like you cannot. If you have any inclination towards being renowned, you best learn how to rub elbows with these influential entities and impress them. Because when you impress them, you impress the world.

Wait! You're shy! You do not want to do the media thing. But you are a writer. You know how to piece words together into soul-altering, mind-bending, tear-jerking phrases that capture people's attention. And those words can touch the media without your personal presence.

You are a writer with powers to influence. Put that power to work and pave your way to media success. Make your words create images that attract readers and the media. The better you write it, present it, and distribute it, the less you have to talk. Make your press activity speak emphatically to garner that media attention for you.

Press Releases

You must know how to write a quality press release. Authors have to spread their own news about a new book, an award or an appearance at a conference. Radios, television stations and Internet sites receive tons of these releases, and yours has to stand out. Your release must tell a story that entices the reader to know more, and will translate into someone attending your signing, conference or award presentation. The press release needs to tell a tale as arresting as any mystery or suspense short story.

Hiring a press agent gives you an edge, but your financial limitations may play a factor. If an agent is not an option, teach yourself the key points of an alluring press release. Do not throw one together with just the facts and expect someone to pick it up and read between the lines that this event might be interesting. Make that release sing a song of success to alleviate the stress of promotion by phone or in person.

Just what do you need in that superior press release? Enough to catch the eye and spill some juicy details before the eye gets tired and leaves. Keep it only one page long – two pages when you have no other choice.

- **Identify the main topic.** Make it short, concise and interesting. Just saying a new book is released doesn't cut it. Saying the book is "an innovative concept for handling the teenager you love to hate and hate to love" says so much more. You do not include your entire writing history in this one page release. But you do tell the media why this topic, this event, is newsworthy right now and how you are the expert on the subject.

- **Identify the 5 W's and an H.** Your high school teacher probably taught you the who, what, when, where, why and how of journalism. Here is where that knowledge pays off. Put a name to each of these descriptors and include them in the first paragraph. Make the headline clear and loud!

- **Speak to the masses.** In case this release prints just as you submitted it, make sure the verbiage caters to the general public. That means no high tech lingo, professional acronyms, or fifty-cent words.

- **Remember the pyramid on its head.** After you created that important opening paragraph with all the W's, an H and the main focal point, elaborate from the most important point down to the least. Assume that the reader will lose interest and put all the important information as close to the top as possible. You convince most people in the first one to two paragraphs, so you cram all the goodies near the top.

- **Facts not flowers.** This is journalism not fiction. Keep the adjectives and adverbs to a minimum. Your release needs to be a grabber, but it does not need to be ornate and sound like an infomercial. This is groundbreaking news, not an ad.

- **Quote.** Someone needs to say something profound. Whether a celebrity recommends your work or you express an outstanding point from your writing, you need "dialogue" as if the reader was listening. It makes the material credible and shows that you are worthy of notice.

- **Factual wrap.** Standard practice places all contact information at the end with maybe a word or two about the background of the writer – you. Brief, very brief.

- **Search.** Look at professional examples before writing a press release of your own. Websites like Marketwire (http://www.marketwire.com), Press Release Writing (http://www.press-release-writing.com), and PRWeb (http://www.prweb.com) not only give good tips but also help organize a release distribution for your event.

- **Send it to the right person.** Shooting out press releases in a shotgun approach may hit a lot of targets, but probably won't bag a kill unless you send it to the right person. With as much paper as the media receives, sending your release to a general location without fine-tuning the correct recipient is futile. They are too darn busy to route your one piece of paper to that one right person whose name is not on the envelope. But they are not too busy to toss it in the can. Notice I mentioned paper and avoided email. Just as you find it easier to send an email release, the media finds it easier to delete them. Stick with paper. Know the individual contacts and include their names at the top with the "For Immediate Release" information.

- **Format.** Double-space for an easier read with 1.5 to 2-inch margins to clearly frame the page. Use no more than four different fonts, sizes, and styles or you gain amateur status or risk looking like a magazine cutout ransom letter. Print the release on letterhead with your logo.

Press releases provide a good avenue for the shy writer. A shrewd and wide distribution of the release opens doors, dodges cold calling, and begs for coverage. You send out your notices and you sit back and wait for the calls to start pouring in. I hope that is the case for you, but unfortunately quick and plentiful responses will not happen. So what else can you do to increase your chances of the publication of your press release, an interview, or a talk show appearance?

Call the people to whom you sent the releases. Thought you got out of that phone call, didn't you? Breaking out in hives just thinking about the calls? Build up a momentum by calling the bank about a deposit, your friend about dinner, and the hardware store about a certain size bolt...then jump right in and call the press release people. You get used to dialing and talking on the phone. As mentioned in an earlier chapter, have your words bulleted or even written verbatim so you do not call speechless or stuttering.

What if selling is not your bag? It isn't mine, either. I despise phones. I let the machine answer for me and caller identification tell me who is calling. I bite the bullet and talk on the damned thing only when absolutely necessary. Option? Have someone call on your behalf. Remember the assistant who aided your book signing and made you look important? Use someone as your representative who loves chatting. My husband has a knack for making people like him, so I use him. He has a nametag with the FundsforWriters logo then under it, "Hope's Husband." He plays along. When I need to make a cold call, I plead with him to do it for me. Sounds mighty official to have "Hope Clark's representative" calling. I draw the line at having him call editors about article content, though. Goodness knows what he would have me writing!

Promo Kit

Often called media kits, these "packets" give your press release three dimensions. As always, the more you give people, the less you have to explain in the day-to-day effort to sell yourself. Make sure your kit's first impression is that of polish, not clutter. Your invisibility, however, means your media kit is that much more important, because it has to speak louder and more succinctly. Include as a minimum:

- **A well-honed press release**. Give it an earth-shattering story or enlightenment about you, your book, or your background. Make it juicy and newsy.

- **A detailed biography**. Avoid the little half page sample or the book jacket blip. Give yourself the mystique the public seeks in a published writer and elaborate about your prestigious, colorful, or successful history. And yes, you do have such a history so paint it as such. The bio is different from the press release information. You want to make the receiver's job easy by educating him quickly so he has absolutely no other research to do about you. When he reads the final sentence, he should feel he has what he needs to proceed with that news article or book review.

- **A story background**. Background information broadcasts why this book cried to be written, printed, and distributed to the masses. What change of heart, personal experience, or chain of events made you pound the keys for months to spread this message? Or, what made you get into the writing business, if you do not have a book? What makes you appear before people in spite of your shyness? Capitalize on anything, including your shyness. Make it draw tears, encourage laughter or shake a head.

- **A fact sheet**. Press folks and a busy public like bullets. List trivia about the book, yourself, your fans, whatever snippets that might catch attention. Author tips, personal secrets, testimonies, recipes, and advice count, too. If you are a nonfiction or commercial writer, the facts cover your services as well. These facts can repeat items from the bio, press release, or other background sources. If you are a romance novelist who studied quantum physics, say so. It catches attention and might nail the review. List these facts as if the recipient only has time to read this one piece of paper.

- **At least two photos and the cover**. The standard head pose speaks as the professional you are. The casual informal pose in a representative setting says you are human. Note how many authors pose with their dogs, their boat, their motorcycle or bare feet on the beach. Pictures reach out and connect. And if you have a candid picture of yourself writing, signing books, or reading, you become the writer in a natural environment everyone wants to see. Add a wine glass or coffee mug and you portray the perfect writer stereotype that others fantasize. Who hasn't wanted to be a writer at some time in his life? Include a big color picture of your book cover in the kit, too.

- **Business cards**. Put at least two cards in the package. Many people keep business cards like an address book. Give them extras to pass around.

- **Freebies**. If you have a pen with your logo, put it in. Postcards, magnets, bookmarks or stickers all work. No one can resist a freebie. But just make it one or you risk sending a packet that looks like a salesman's sample case.

- **Your book or article**. Expect to give away a certain number of books to entice reviews and coverage. A book copy tempts the reviewer, but prioritize your distribution to those who more likely say yes, or those who reach the largest public. Send press releases or promo kits coupled with your book and someone might bite. At the very least include the first chapter or two as a teaser. Autograph a book copy to give it extra appeal and make the recipient feel guilty about tossing your request to the side (or in the trashcan). The signature gives it extra value and attracts second looks. If your forte is articles, short stories, poetry or essays, include clips. Let them see actual published pieces. And awards speak for themselves so mention them.

- **Reviews**. If you have a particularly brilliant review of your work, by all means stick it in your kit. Testimonials from satisfied customers laud your expertise as a commercial or copywriter. A third party's praise goes a lot further than self-acclaim.

- **An online website press room**. Make sure the above and more are online. Have your book signing tour route listed, more testimonials, samples of your writing and anything else that connects with you. Put that website address on anything and everything you hand out. If you want to avoid the face-to-face, you make your online world compensate.

Interviews

Sooner or later you give an interview. Some writer will want to know how you got where you are. Or a student wonders what it is like to be a writer. And if you publish a great book, maybe... just maybe...you will receive requests from radio and television stations. And goodness knows the Web abounds with interviews in newsletters and on websites. Scary? Any of the above gives most writers the jitters.

In general, the best way to handle all of these interviews is preparation. Ask for the questions in advance, answer them on paper, send them back to the interviewer, and keep a copy for yourself. The process of typing the responses plants the answers in your head. Regardless of the type of interview, this method works. You think about the sound of the responses, reword them, consider their impact, and even discard ideas you might not have if you had been asked impromptu. Your credibility is everything so you are entitled to think about your words beforehand.

I always require advance questions. Granted, I understand that once the interviewer reads my answers she might change the next question, but I do ask that they keep the conversation in line with the questions – at least in general. No one has refused me yet.

Preparing yourself in this manner does amazing things to your memory and speech. You recall what you typed as if you engraved it directly on your gray matter. Your speech flows because your mind does not have to work as hard. The pauses, um's and er's that break the flow of oral presentations decrease or vanish. Those fillers are needed to give the brain time to sort data and words before the mouth spits them out. If you prepared the brain, the mouth follows suit. Suddenly the interview is over, and you wonder where the time disappeared.

Now we cover the different types of interviews you face as a serious writer.

- **Email** – I adore these! Online writers and even glossy magazine writers often send the questions via email asking for answers by return email. No pressure whatsoever. Take your time and write with style and verve. Read it back aloud. Now aren't you inspiring? That is because you are!

- **Online Chats** – I did a couple of these recently and had an absolute ball. A good moderator makes a difference and if you are the key speaker in the chat, you need a moderator. Even if the chat is your design under your name, have a third party to keep the questions coordinated and at bay. Ever visited a chat room where conversations flew everywhere in all directions? People had to name the person they were talking to because six chats were taking place all at once.

  Even for online chats I ask for some insight on where the moderator intends to direct the conversation. A good moderator will have questions of his own (and your answers) just in case he needs fillers, people are shy, or the talk detours off topic. If he does not ask for questions and answers, send him some. Be prepared to type fast during the chat and concentrate. Even have some pat sentences in a Word document on your computer in case you like to cut and paste short blips about your work, book, web or sales. Think before answering off the cuff when a unique question comes your way.

  I once participated in an online chat that flowed well with all the players having fun. Suddenly a question zinged my way – perfectly innocent. "What do you think about critique groups?" "Personally," I said, "I hate them."

Too much opinion too quick, I learned. The moderator held regular critique groups on several writing levels, and I was a guest on his site! Once the group laughed and identified that fact, I replied that a good critique moderator was awful hard to find, and once you found one, you should treat him like a precious jewel and cherish the opportunity. Whew! I rebounded and everyone was happy with the moderator now identified as a superb critique leader. I felt like a heel, but the chat rolled on without disturbance and with lots of chuckles. Glad no one physically saw me because I blushed crimson.

If I had done my homework, I would have visited the chat room in advance and learned that the atmosphere was jovial, even comical. Members pick on each other in jest making the event fun and pull the guest into the banter. Keep your professional face on and watch for the innocent zinger. Five seconds of sarcasm can erode your image.

- **Telephone** – Telephone interviews tense my shoulders a bit until I achieve a comfort level with the interviewer. You do not see the person, but you can feel her presence. In person you can tell if the recipient heard your words or understood your meaning with the subtle nuances of eyebrow, mouth and hands, but on the phone you have no signals. You can depart on a tangent and miss a subtle point.

    Alleviate these problems with questions prepared in advance and your answers before you. Wear comfortable clothes and give yourself space to move around. Staying seated during the entire interview can feel confining; walking and open space gives you room to not only vent energy but also express yourself more naturally. I am a pacer. When I talk to someone I walk, wave my arms, and slide papers. Like I explained in a previous chapter, I hate telephones, and combining that with sitting leads my mind to wander. I catch myself wishing the ordeal would hurry and end.

So I interview in my kitchen. My interview answers are spread out side-by-side on the counter. With pen in hand, I mark off the questions as they occur. This activity helps me measure the progression of the interview and double-check my answers against my preparations. Often I become the culprit who deviates from the questions, but at least having them before me helps rein me in.

My pen jots ideas as they occur. Balancing a formal interview of prepared questions while dealing with a fleeting flash of brilliance is challenging, so I doodle comments. I do this so I do not interrupt the interviewer – a real no-no. On the phone, you often cannot tell when the other party has ended a thought. Be a keen listener. Using the advance questions and answers technique helps you identify when a thought is complete. Do not ramble, but instead make a clear point with an obvious ending letting the other person know when to speak. Answer the question and stop. Hopefully you have done as I suggested earlier and sent your written answers to the interviewer ahead of time. He will realize when you complete a thought and make the interview more enjoyable with no surprises. But use the answers as guides or bullets only, since reading verbatim sounds rote and mechanical.

- **Radio –** These can be fun if you let them. A good host makes you forget about listeners numbering in the thousands. You carry on a conversation, and before you know it you are signing off and thanking your host. A radio interview can take place via telephone or in person. Either way, the process is usually taped. That means mistakes are allowed and cut out. Taping beats online chats where the verbal horse might escape out of the barn and there is no getting it back. If you grow tongue-tied, ask to stop and regroup. You feel better and the host will have a better interview.

I once performed an interview where the radio recording person was in one state, the host resided in another and I lived in yet another. The host graciously honored my advance question request and stuck tightly to the list making the interview smooth as silk. We finished the interview, I let out a sigh of relief and giggled with the host while the tech guy checked something. Suddenly the guy cuts in and says, "Hey ladies, I need you to revisit question two and do it again. We've got a problem on the tape." Off the top of my head I couldn't think of question two, but thank goodness we both had our notes. She was a charmer and stepped right into character asking the question again. My momentum was not as fluid as hers so I started reading the answer with as much conviction as possible until I could regain my footing. After two sentences, I was back on track. But I counted my lucky stars that I had those answers in black and white on my kitchen counter!

But what if...just what if...the interviewer wants an impromptu interview. No questions in advance! Oh, dear!

You can opt out of the interview, stress firmly that you need those questions in advance to keep your act together, or you can require that a pre-briefing be arranged so you can become acquainted with the interview and conversationally discuss what the interview will cover. Your comfort level with interviews determines your choice. A good interviewer will make you feel more at ease after a short chat and let you realize you are not a movie celebrity someone is trying to blindside with embarrassing questions. And always remember, you are the expert of your writing material, which makes you more knowledgeable about the topic anyway.

You are the guest so let the interviewer run the show. Do not worry about dead space or timing because the professional will edit, cut and prepare the interview for the air. Answer questions and wait for the host to pull you along with her subtle direction. Filling in space is her job. And talk to *her*, not the audience. The room probably houses just the two of you so treat the conversation like an afternoon coffee. As happened with my interview above, the host did just what she was supposed to do – made it all come together.

- **Television** – Chances are, your television appearance is taped so throw shyness to the wind. Go prepared, as always. The fact that your face, clothes and body will greet thousands of people does give you pause. Preparation, preparation, and preparation. Chances are, you will not answer more than a half-dozen questions. Commercials, introductions, introductions of the commercials, conclusion and reminders about the next show take up half the airtime.

  Dress simple but professional. If you are not sure how to prepare, call and ask. They will give you pointers. If you feel antsy during the interview and need some consolation, or a pacifier as I call it, grab your book or a pen to keep your hands from waving and wandering. Settle comfortably in your seat beforehand and plant your butt. Wiggling like a four-year-old implies nerves, neophyte and inexperience. If saying so will not damage the image you are trying to promote, say you are nervous. Often times it dispels some of the edginess and settles you down to the task at hand.

  Want to know something else that helps dissolve those nerves? Look the interviewer straight in the eye. Letting your own eyes wander says you are uncomfortable, not only in the setting but in talking about the subject matter. Focusing on the interviewer makes you address him and forget about the environment. It gives you purpose and direction. That interviewer becomes your audience, so educate and enlighten him in a one-on-one session. Feeling in control, in tune and in touch with yourself gives you energy.

  And remember, like the audiences that want to see you succeed, most interviewers wish the same. After all, your success makes them look sharp and sound smart.

  If you face a severe case of stage fright, ask to share the show. Bring an assistant who helped you do research, another author with a like book, a person with a similar experience to the one in your book, or a pleased customer who benefited from your writing. A three-way or four-way conversation removes the intense pressure from you. Those earlier six questions probably reduce to three. Scared to ask them to make this innovative adjustment? Have your trusty personal assistant with the people skills and gutsy flare give them a call and make the request.

- **Real Time Anything**

    You are the guest, and the interviewer is the host. Go to the interview prepared with your homework fresh in your mind and let the host lead. Answer with short sentences to avoid errors, letting the interviewer fill in any gaps. He will! He does this kind of thing for a living so let him do his job. He guides you right through the ordeal. So what if you suddenly display a verbal stumble. As long as you avoid four-letter words, slanderous accusations, and competitive mud-slinging, your stutter probably will endear you to the audience.

The Interviewer in You

Time to turn the tables. Many freelance writers need interview subjects with some specializing in unique and quality exchanges with colorful, professional, and famous people. Barbara Walters has a way with interviews and while we would faint dead away if placed in her shoes, we can at least copy some of her winning techniques.

Interviews vary in style and technique. Face-to-face raises the stress meter a bit while emailed questions provide ease and simplicity. The shy writer opts for email interviews every chance she gets. The outgoing freelancer thrives for more one-on-one to capitalize on tangential conversation. A middle ground exists with telephone and live online chats.

As the interviewer you represent the host, regardless of the medium. You hold the responsibility of covering the material while making the interviewee feel comfortable. But you also owe both your editor and guests a first-rate performance.

- **In person.** Dress professionally. Try for comfort, but appearance and impression count more when you are leading the show. Make sure the other person is relaxed, as an awkward guest makes for a less than congenial exchange. Offer heartfelt thanks at the beginning and at the end. Good manners prevail at all times. Treat the guest of honor like royalty. Walk the person through the interview format asking in advance for any issues of preference or deference. Make the event painless for him as if you were in his shoes under the lights. Nervous? Practice, practice, and practice your questions alone, before a mirror, on a tape recorder, and with a substitute person. Watch and listen to yourself. Ask your substitute guest for feedback. Remember how preparation reduces stress.

- **Telephone.** Whew, toss the pantyhose or tie aside. Look at earlier guidance about being interviewed and change chairs. Send your questions in advance. But the smart interviewer also asks for the answers in advance to aid the interview progress. Make your sentences clear with obvious endings so they can easily read your cues.

- **Online chat.** For the introvert, this method does relieve pressure. But beware of nimble fingers and quick pinkies on the "enter" key. Have questions prepared. When tangents occur, think a second before spouting back a quick retort or query. Make sure you understand the meaning and display courtesy and respect in your wording. Online correspondence lacks the emotional cues of telephone and face-to-face interviews. Consider prompts like [more] and [done] when the two of you are exchanging thoughts. Such prearranged hints keep the conversation on topic, avoid interruption, and prevent a dozen criss-crossing thoughts.

- **Email.** Email is best for simple interviews. Since emails are one-way, bundled exchanges, and tangents have less chance to occur. Establish whether you can contact the interviewee for subsequent questions that may arise from the first interview. Always do your homework beforehand to avoid asking mundane or embarrassing questions. Since you may not have multiple chances to fine-tune your questions later, strive for the best ones up front. Because the ordeal is simple does not give you the latitude to shortcut your mental investment in the questions.

Providing simple courtesies to an interviewed person helps the interview process. His ease and comfort with you work like a reflection; you relax as well. And regardless of the interview method, detailed preparation diminishes pressure. Paying attention to your research, your writing, your looks, your composure, and your comfort lessen the urge to retreat. Not only do you focus on something other than your fear, but you gain confidence in knowing what to expect.

The press and the media are a must for an author. You might be able to handle promotion through other avenues and avoid the ears and eyes of radio and television, but remember that the more successful you become, the more people want to see and hear you. Indeed a Catch-22 situation. A writer creates worlds, sways opinion and tells stories. If you can conquer the imagination, you can handle shyness and its obstacles. Remember, the more inhibited you are, the more creative you must become in adjusting the situation to suit you.

Become so wrapped up in something that you forget to be afraid.

~Lady Bird Johnson

Chapter 10
Other People Power

- Start With Relatives
- Friends Are Fun
- Familiar Acquaintances Work Well, Too
- Distant Acquaintances
- Reviews
- Requests
- Order Blanks
- People Power

Each person has strengths. No man or woman truly stands alone in his or her success. An accomplished writer reaches the pinnacle not only with individual strengths but also through the support of others: a publisher, a literary agent, a spouse, press agents, bookstore managers, as well as fans, readers and customers. No person is an island. As reclusive as you may be, you need the efforts of others to sell your writing.

The more outgoing person likes leading the show and taking center stage on this path to achievement. But the shy writer has the inclination and savvy to include the strengths of others to help climb that ladder of fortune if for no other reason than to avoid performing herself. You may envision yourself a hermit, but you do touch other people. You connect with some who could be your networking aides every week, if not daily.

Start With Relatives

Pretend you need an invitation list for a wedding, graduation, baby announcement, or retirement event, and note all of your relations. They do not have to be next door or across town. The uncle in Michigan can sing your praises as much as the niece in New York.

Create an announcement package for your book, your column, or your magazine feature for your relatives about your expected publication. In your package, include bookmarks, postcards, business cards and press release just as you would for a radio station or news editor. Any freebies you would hand out to your fans, you can give to your relatives. You might even consider a gift designed especially for family. The extra freebies you refrained from including in your earlier promo package are quite appropriate here.

In addition, include a personal note from you. Capitalize on this opportunity to reconnect with them. Ask them, with lots of gracious thank-yous, to use the package to broadcast the news in their area, in their circle of friends and acquaintances. Tell them they have a published writer in the family, and you would love for them to use their bragging rights.

If you can afford to do so, send a copy of your book – autographed. Your aunt will tell her whole church about her nephew the author and probably pull the book from her purse to show the Sunday school class. And grandparents brag until they are hoarse about a 'famous' grandchild. Follow up on their need for a second round of bookmarks and giveaways for the garden club or PTO.

These people have your best interest in mind more than anyone on the planet. They may not understand a thing in your book, but they will brag about your ability to write and publish. Their friends, neighbors, business partners, and co-workers will take their word for it that you are great and lend a hand to the cause. Think of it as selling Girl Scout cookies. Many a Girl Scout set sales records because of a network of relatives. I know I did.

My mother worked in a hospital steno-pool back in the days before computers. My father was in the Air Force. I could go to either office during cookie sales time and sell an obscene amount of thin mint and peanut butter sandwich cookies. I won a trip to camp for the summer and I believe my mother still has the newspaper clipping announcing my sales record.

Remember I was shy – painfully so as a youngster. But by asking my relatives to help, I achieved awards and acclaim for my sales. Why should that united effort stop once you write for a living? They still love you and want you to succeed.

Finally, to avoid looking like an opportunistic distant relative, follow up with subsequent correspondence. Keep them active in your address book. Add them to your newsletter, and spotlight their help! Remember that manners and courtesy go a long way in this world of dog-eat-dog competition. And that includes your family.

Friends Are Fun

Give friends your promo package. Using themed announcements, have a party where you hand them the packages in a grand gesture. Run a contest where the pal who sells the most books or signs up the most newsletter subscribers wins dinner on you. This is not a formal release gala where you meet and greet strangers. Make it a cookout, pizza party, poker night, or pool party where you enjoy those closest to you while expanding your customer base.

Order tee shirts and coffee cups with your logo, book cover, or website and present them with the condition that your friends flaunt them. Consider affiliate relationships where you allow your friends to make commissions from sales that they orchestrated. Watch the fun begin.

Your friends and associates have connections to others outside your circle. And these in turn connect to other circles. As a result, the contacts can range far and wide beyond your imagination. Feed these people with promotional material worth distributing (not hand cut copies on pink construction paper), and they will tout your praises to people you cannot imagine. You never know when a friend will conveniently touch base with a business acquaintance who needs a self-help manual for his 150 employees. Surely you have a few boisterous, friendly and effervescent amigos who connect with people much more easily than you do.

Again remember the gratitude. Throw another party or send thank-you notes to these pals who helped you reach your pinnacle of success.

Familiar Acquaintances Work Well, Too

Now comes a different list of assistants. I call them familiar acquaintances and they consist of those you see regularly. Individuals that comprise this list can be:

- **Co-workers**. Remember the Girl-Scout cookies? You buy their child's wrapping paper so they feel inclined to buy your book.

- **Club members.** The writing group, the garden club, or the PTA. All have publications, newsletters, or bulletin boards.

- **Sports.** From Little League Baseball and amateur hockey to bowling teams and jogging races you know a lot of these people, players, coaches, and fans. Know anyone connected with minor league or semi-pro sports? Call in a favor. Author and humor columnist Karen Rinehart plastered her name and book cover for *Invisible Underwear, Bus Stop Mommies and Other Things True to Life* on the side of a NASCAR vehicle at the Busch Grant National. She obviously knew someone to pull that off. See it at http://www.karenrinehart.net/BSM_Photos.html.

- **Charities.** You have supported a particular local charity for years, and they thank you often. Ask for a favor in return, even if it is just a mention in their next mailing.

Offer them a percentage of profits for a certain sales period or for a particular event openly displaying your united effort to raise funds. Instead of paying a sponsor fee, offer proceeds from your sales in exchange for your name on their banners, shirts, brochures, and ads. Belong to an arts organization or writers group? Why not have a day where the members gather to sell their wares with a percentage going to the club, foundation, or nonprofit? You demonstrate how generous and civic-minded you are to your customers.

- **Schools.** Teachers are supportive souls by nature who love to spread the news about books and writing, especially regarding a student or parent they know. And if you are an alumnus of an educational institution, submit your press in the next alumni publication through an article about your new book or syndicated column.

- **Medical contacts.** Dentist, orthodontist, gynecologist, podiatrist, internist, family doctor, veterinarian, or dermatologist, the possibilities are endless. Ask if you can stand a book on their counter or leave a stack of bookmarks with ordering information. I kidded my dentist into supporting my son's extracurricular sport activities in lieu of buying a new golf club, and he gave a handsome sum. Then I had a plaque made to hang in his waiting room for all the patients to see. Such a wall adornment costs maybe $10 but the effort praises your sponsor and gives you additional advertising.

- **Local shops.** If you have lived in an area for a few years, you know the neighborhood storeowners. Ask them to display your wares or at least post your cards and bookmarks. Offer commissions. And do not forget consignment shops. You will find the best sales occur in shops that touch upon your theme – a business guide in an office supply, a children's book in a toy store, or an outdoorsy novel in a sports outlet.

- **Hairdresser.** How many items have you seen displayed in a beauty shop, nail salon or spa? Clothes, purses, scarves, jewelry, hair products, coffee, exotic drinks, health food, even pet products can be found in these places where people gather to make themselves more attractive. I bake pecan pies for my hairdresser and I know she'd buy a book from me or at least post my display in her store regardless of the subject. My mother could sell anything through her regular beauty shop where she has been coifed for over twenty years! Same goes for your barber, manicurist, gym, or YMCA.

- **Chamber of Commerce.** This compilation of community movers and shakers represents powerful buying dollars. The Chamber itself will broadcast your success if you are a member. With one or two members admiring your work, you can expect the word or your talents to spread like wildfire. Speak at the monthly luncheon and great opportunities may happen when other businesses see the potential of your work helping their profits or their employees' morale.

- **Car dealers.** I purchased three cars from the same dealer in the span of five years. I asked him to support my son's hockey team and walked away with $500. The dealer felt obligated to assist me because of my loyalty to him. Take an accounting of other "loyalty" connections in your hometown and call in the favors.

- **Miscellaneous events**. And what does this mean? It means anywhere that people who know you may gather in your community like the county fair, the walkathon for cancer, or even the senior prom if your book can fit into a theme for teens. You may have self-published your book and cannot get a major bookstore to display it. But I bet you can talk an independent bookstore into accepting it if you combine your signing with a jazz or classical band ensemble, finger foods, and local artists- all with CDs, books and art to sell. Make it a cultural event during October – National Arts and Humanities Month. That major bookstore just might change its mind, and you may start an annual event for your hometown.

Most people prefer doing business with repeat customers. As the shy member of my family, my husband is the connection to our business acquaintances. I know a few, but he seems to open doors so much easier than I do. As a result, our family's business acquaintances tend to remember me via his identity. So when I need something, I often ask him to make the contact. Whether you, your spouse, your son, or your significant other shakes the hand, use that impression to sell your writing. Your dedication to that business, person, or organization reaps a reward in return when you ask for likewise support.

Distant Acquaintances

Take this concept as far as you want to take it. The point is to think of each and every contact as a potential sale. As a shy person you are not likely to appear ostentatious or overbearing, so I have no concern that you might develop a used-car-salesman mentality; however, the attitude of a salesman that *every person is a customer* works in your favor.

- **Mail.** Possible promotion exists through the utility bill, the garbage collection, the car payment, the tuition payment, the pest control company, the furniture bill, the hospital medical charges, the charity donation, the catalog order, your income tax 'contribution,' your article submission, and so on. If you lick a stamp for it, promote through it. Keep promotional information next to your stamps and stuff every envelope with a business card or bookmark.

- **Exchange business cards.** You have had people hand you their business card. Hand them one right back with the ordering information for your book or services. And when the sales people come to your door? Turn the tables and get them to walk away with your book. Offer to buy his product if he buys yours. When you write a check, hand someone your card, freebie, or bookmark at the same time. A little subtle bartering never hurts.

- **Newspaper.** When you renew the paper, send an article in the payment envelope asking the editor to consider your piece, press release, or public announcement.

- **Your daily path.** Eat lunch at the café? Leave a bookmark. Get your car's oil changed? Hand them a card. Buy a greeting card? Leave your postcard. Everywhere you get up from a seat in a waiting room, airport, theatre, or restaurant, leave your mark Move about well armed with your promotional material, and always have a book on hand. You just might sell it. You do not have to make a big production out of it, but you can leave a trail of who you are wherever you go. FundsforWriters adorns my checks, and during one bank visit the teller asked me what that meant. When I explained what I did for a living, he asked for my card. That evening I probably had another visitor to the website and a subscriber to at least one newsletter.

Reviews

An underutilized tool, the book review can add momentum to sales. Flaunt any commendations or accolades. Your book, your newsletter, your article or your column all merit reviews. Organized word-of-mouth carries far. Good reviews sell.

Send copies of your book to respected individuals and ask for feedback and testimonials before the book is published. Use the best quotes over and over again. Plaster them on the book jacket. Write articles? Expecting a piece in a national glossy magazine?

Send them to a few notable names and collect the endorsements for your promo kit, website, and press release.

Publishing a newsletter? Ask for membership opinion, post it online, and include in your promo kit. Writing commercial copy? Give each client an opinion form to complete and return.

Writers serve each other loyally. If they can aid one another, they will. Pick out your writing buddies and ask for reviews. Have them submit their comments not only to you but also to Amazon and other websites. Look to your peers and learn to exchange advise, information, and promotion. I would not hesitate to ask a handful of newsletter editors for assistance because they know I would be there for them in return.

Ask editors to mention you on their web sites. You find announcement postings in newsletters like Write Success (http://www.writesuccess.com) and the international Burryman (http://www.burryman.com). Professional writing groups like Romance Writers of America, Mystery Writers of America, and The Poetry Society, flaunt member accomplishments. Stop and think where you read about other writers, then post your own reviews and testimonials (or ask others to post on your behalf if that is the protocol).

All of this online activity sounds so much louder that your little bitty voice. Emailing others is a relief for the shy writer. I'm an email devotee. I am more apt to ask a favor of a well-known author online than in person. I type and hit "send" any day over picking up the phone or knocking on a door.

Requests

Let us digress from the reviews and look at requests. Radio stations take requests from listeners. Ever watch those music video shows where viewers call in opinions or vote for songs? Now is where your friends and relatives come in handy again.

Of course, they hand out your material here and there, but they can do more to carry your promotion a bit further. Ask them to talk about you, ask about you, or make a plea for you. Make these people your mini-agents. They can perform these tasks on your behalf:

- **Radio.** They can call or write the radio stations asking for your book to be featured on the next literary talk show.

- **Television.** They can call or write television stations, shows, and individual hosts asking for attention for your new book, column, or website business.

- **Libraries.** They can ask that the library carry your book. Have five friends ask in a two-week period and that book will appear on the shelf. Libraries have budgets and buy books just like bookstores.

- **Bookstores.** Have three friends request your book, and the manager may order ten to meet the sudden demand. Later, walk into the store and ask for a book signing. Or solicit the owner to set up a display so you forego the public appearance, if you prefer.

- **Letters to the paper.** Imagine letters to the editor about a good book instead of gas prices, war, the economy, and politics. Ask a friend to write one for your book, column, or copywriting business. Such letters grab attention if coordinated with timely news or entertainment releases that parallel your material.

- **Educational requests.** Asking the PTA or the school board to consider a new children's book might succeed if the request comes from a dozen different parents. PTA's are nonprofit organizations, and some have more funds that you think.

- **Amazon.** Request relatives, friends, and cohorts write a few words about your book on Amazon. While some authors question the credibility of this review process, buyers still read the reviews. I know I do.

- **Online reviews.** You have online writer friends. They would write a dignified review of your work. Maybe you do not have a book, but you write a column, publish a newsletter, or manage a website. A critique works in these arenas, too. Newsletter and website editors are always seeking well-written analyses. Plead with your buddies to provide sparkling evaluations and spread them far and wide on the Internet.

- **Reading groups and writer clubs.** Ask friends to request you as a guest for their organization with the condition you can sell your services afterwards. Have them request your book's presentation at the next meeting. Want good feedback before it's printed? Ask that the group analyze your pre-published or galley-level work to catch mistakes. As a local author, they might jump at the chance to be your advisors. My son had a college professor who wrote a technical manual for a computer class. Before it was published, he used the book in class as required reading and asked the students to edit each chapter as it was covered. What an innovative way to spread the word about a book and receive free editing at the same time from a room of subject-interested readers.

The list goes on and on. Have the people you know campaign and make requests for your writing. Politicians have campaigners – so can you.

Order Blanks

Never leave a customer wondering how to place an order. From miniature order blanks on postcards and bookmarks to order forms in the book itself, have the address, price, website, and phone number handy.

Design creative ordering formats. Make them cute, easy to read, handy, enticing, neat and professional. Your people power distribution becomes easier when you have the information right there in their hands. Your shy friend might not tell colleagues how to order, but she can sure hand out a tasteful, art-graphic postcard with the form on the back.

Some argue that printing on the back of business cards is amateurish and others call it frugal. But if your information is on the front and the order blank on the back, I call it smart marketing. Keep the ordering process simple so it fits on anything.

People Power

People talking, exchanging, interacting, and socializing provide the best source of advertising you could ask for. Take inventory of your advertising potential by labeling each person in your world as a distribution tool. You thereby delegate that horrendous task called marketing to others. Call it respect for their abilities instead of taking advantage. Besides, you would be glad to help them in return. Ask them to buy your thin mint cookies knowing that later you will be asked to support their grand-opening, fundraiser, or chocolate bar sales campaign. We are each other's support and each other's customers.

I am not afraid of storms,
for I am learning how to sail my ship.

~*Louisa May Alcott*

Chapter 11
Controversy – When Shy Doesn't Work

- When Shyness Does Not Work
- Negative in the Crowd
- The Writers Group
- Judge the Necessity of Appearance
- Calm Yourself

If life could slide by without an obstacle, we'd all be happy, warm and fuzzy. But life does not work that way, plus the bumps along the way develop character. An old boss of mine once advised me with that thought, and boy, have I developed a lot of character! Looking back, those ordeals made me into a better person even though the ride gave me bruises.

Shyness hurts at times and we often prefer to be left alone than confronted about it. But shyness has no place in some settings. What you must develop is a threshold where the shyness stops and assertiveness steps in. And you do have an assertive side when the right occasion arises.

We all set this threshold based on personal preferences. I know a few folks who tossed "shy" out of their vocabulary a long time ago. They strut into just about any setting and deal with it. Some charismatic people live for an exhibition, a party or a public forum. They shine in front of crowds, yet struggle when they are left alone to handle a dilemma. The shy person already knows to think first and act second. So 'think' about dealing with public situations.

When Shyness Does Not Work

Place an extrovert in a quandary surrounded by people and he will handle it on the spot and be thrilled doing it. Place an introvert in the same situation and he will find a way to handle it alone. In some cases one is better than the other. When is being shy not acceptable?

- **Contract negotiations**. In the nitty-gritty business of legal matters, the shy and modest lose the battle, the rights, and the money on the table. In laymen's terms, they get "taken to the cleaners." A shy writer dealing with book contracts needs to find an professional agent or learn assertiveness training. Agents thrive on contract negotiations and my suggestion is to find a good one to hone those publishing contracts.

  But what if you write freelance articles? You learn the business and speak up for your rights. A shy writer unable to bargain is shark bait. She can expect to lose many of the perks that go with being a freelance writer. She fights an uphill battle unless she speaks up and asks for one-time rights instead of exclusive, or 50 cents a word instead of 25. If she does not ask, she does not receive.

  Once again, you might consider a representative to speak on your behalf. Just make sure that the representative knows what she is doing. The spouse that draws customers to your book signing or arranges interviews might not understand first North American serial rights from foreign serial rights or one-time rights from serial rights. Losing ownership of your beloved words can be critical both emotionally as well as professionally, not to mention financially.

  You need a voice with a brain when negotiating a contract. Find one. And if you can't, then speak up for yourself. Being shy in such a setting tells the other side that you work for cheap.

- **Business communication.** Regardless of how reserved you are, forgetting or declining to return phone calls and emails is bad manners and poor business etiquette. The easiest way to scare away customers or insult readers is to ignore them. Set yourself a goal of responding to all contacts within 24 hours. If you receive way too much correspondence to keep that schedule, then set one a bit more realistic, but honor it. Your customers and readers should feel comfortable in that you respect their interest, their opinions, and their support of you. They are your career.

- **Others need you.** You identified yourself as an expert to sell your writing, but connecting with those new protégés makes your knees shake. An expert is no one without a following. You opened the dialogue through your newsletters, books and articles, so keep up the image and spread your knowledge. That means returning calls, emails, talking and even making the occasional presentation. Presenting yourself as a professional then dropping out of sight (or never showing up!) disappoints readers. You do not have to lead a lecture circuit, but somewhere, sometime let people see a face. In today's world of computer cameras, satellite television, and visual telephones, customers expect to know what you look and sound like.

- **Critique groups.** If you belong to a writers group that offers critiques, being shy ranks with rude. You must give and take and involve yourself in the process. Keeping the group small makes it easier for you to speak and subject yourself to criticism, but do not submit without offering supporting advice and do not advise without subjecting yourself to evaluation.

- **When it impacts your self-worth.** If shyness makes you think less of yourself, then it is time to combat it. Shyness as a natural characteristic is fine, but shyness that erodes self-image is not acceptable. To promote yourself as a writer, you need self-confidence and an ability to sell yourself – even if it's creatively from behind the scenes. Feel positive about yourself. Very few people have your attributes. You are unique with many beautiful and wise thoughts to offer others.

- **Social phobia.** When contacting people makes you ill, you have exceeded shy and entered another realm. Seek professional help. Writer or not, being phobic about social settings to the point of remaining indoors and away from all people and places is detrimental to your health and your family's well-being. You might start with Anxieties.com where author and doctor Reid Wilson, PhD lists his books, free self-help courses, and references for additional help. The Anxiety Disorders Association of America offers tips for coping with life's hurdles as well (http://www.adaa.org).

Negative in the Crowd

I believe the worst fear of a shy person is that of being ridiculed in public. That apprehension creates the fear of public speaking adopted by so many people. For some reason we feel that getting up before others subjects us to harassment.

Stop and think. When you listen to a speaker, do you want to embarrass him? As a silent type you would not ask the scalding question or make the slanderous comment. But would you appreciate anyone else chastising the speaker? In all the public forums you have attended, do you remember situations where an audience intimidated the speaker? Outside of political forums which breed heated opinions, or government and school board meetings that air differences, can you name one event where the speech went awry and the speaker slinked away defeated? Bet you cannot recall a single incident.

An audience hopes a speaker succeeds. The listener wishes she could be as bold and silently roots for the orator's overwhelming triumph. And if an audience member attempts a derogatory remark, just watch the rest of the crowd. Frowns, moans, and signs of disapproval flash across faces as they condemn the individual with the poor taste to insult the guest.

But I am playing the devil's advocate here, and since you are reading this book to deal with adversities faced by the shy writer, let's look at ways to confront the potential opposition in your crowd.

- **Predict the unpredictable**. You know your topic matter better than anyone in the room. What would anyone take issue with? Make your list of potentially controversial topics. Then ask a friend or relative to think of the negatives hidden in your presentation. Prepare some short, generic answers and keep them handy. I would write them down and keep them in a separate pocket, just in case. Remember I believe in pockets. They hide a lot of tricks, solutions and nervous energy. As always, preparation is the best combatant against anything stressful.

- **Straddle the fence**. Someone may push your emotional hot button, inadvertently or intentionally. Problem is, if you take a side one way or another, you risk alienating others in the room. When a question starts "In your opinion..." let your radar tell you that this is the time to straddle that fence. Tell the person that the question is sensitive. This respects them for asking but protects your image. Take a breath and give a benign answer unless you are willing to tackle the next escalated question or you are confident in your response.

  Remember when I told the moderator I hated critique groups only to find out he ran one? I answered an "in your opinion" question. Frankly, your feelings mean little in the grand scheme of life, so you are safer and more prudent to give an answer that stands as neutral. "I personally dislike critique groups, but I know some writers who swear by them and believe they improve their craft." There, you protected both sides of the equation. Place no blame and sling no negatives. You are the good guy, and they feel relieved you did not chastise them. Win-win.

- **The unknown**. Sometimes you do not know the answer. Say so. If you feel it is within your power to find the answer, offer to do so and get back in touch with the individual. Be sure to do it. Do not be afraid to admit what you don't know. The group will respect your honesty, plus, the new knowledge gives you fodder for new articles and books.

- **The temptation of the adversary**. In a casual party or social gathering the talk may turn to a topic about which you have strong feelings. To avoid the limelight, your safest bet is to listen and quietly bask in the knowledge that you believe differently, know differently, and feel confident in your stand.

  The composition of the crowd, however, does make a difference. If these are friends in whom you can confide, then you might enjoy the debate. As a quiet person, you probably would not open your mouth unless the group was close-knit anyway. But if the room consists of writers, and these writers invited you to participate in the day's event, be politically smart and maintain a protected stance. You have nothing to gain in expressing a weighty opinion in most of these cases and everything to lose if you upset someone with alternate beliefs. And if these opinions become tempting in a more formal crowd such as a conference, by all means do not express an opinion that potentially will alienate a large number of customers.

  You are a salesperson here. Your personal beliefs are not for airing anymore than your preferences in the bedroom, and regardless of the side you take, you will upset someone.

- **Blatant confrontation**. A couple of times in your life, someone will get in your face, invade your space, and challenge you. I doubt you will see this happen at a writer's convention, book fair, signing or club meeting. Writers are predominantly an open-minded lot - free speech and all that. They tend to be thinkers and not confronters. Sure, one may grab your elbow and pull you aside to contest your views in chapter four of your book, but that's what you want. That means people are digesting your words.

  But just assume someone has one drink too many and protests loudly about how you addressed gay marriage, politics, adultery, abuse, animal rights, or whatever, in chapter three of your book or paragraph twelve in the newspaper feature you published last weekend. Face the fact you will blush. That only makes you human. Chances are the group will intervene in some fashion and deter the protestor. But what if someone asks a testy question and you are left standing there to deal with it? What do you do?

  First, you stay calm.

  Second, be gracious and say you would be glad to discuss it at another time in another setting. Look away or turn around to break the connection. Standing firm just invites more dialogue.

  Third, walk away.

The Southern culture in America has a way of dealing with public adversity. It's called "killing with kindness". Always with a smile, replies are ever in the positive and with concern, but never in a manner that openly chastises. "Bless your heart" can mean just what it says – a personal wish of well being, or a hidden disparagement meaning the poor soul just cannot help himself. The lesson is that manners are first and foremost and that should be your aim. You experience less stress and make those around you breathe a lot easier. Plus, you gain considerable respect from those on the sidelines!

The Writers Group

Some writers love them, others despise them, but writers groups exist in every library and bookstore in America and most of the world. Some discuss books and others share promotional tips. Many cover current trends in publishing and others get down and dirty into the world of critiques.

Shop for a writers group like you would a family doctor, agent, or financial broker. The personality has to fit snug, like a glove. It should feel natural and comforting, encouraging and beneficial. If you cannot open up before the group, the experience is worthless.

- **The good group**. I believe that a good critique group evades most writers. You almost have to start your own group, unless you stumble into a rare and marvelous opportunity. Find those special writers whose work you appreciate, personality you enjoy, and writing you admire, then start a clique. Go to an established writers group and get to know the people. Once you find two or three that rub you the right way, ask them to form a critique group. Do not confuse a writers' group with a critique group as they are usually two different animals.

  Keep the number small so you accomplish genuine work. A dozen writers in a critique group can mean weeks between turns of giving and receiving criticism. The effort of running the group wears it out, and with the large number of people you increase the odds of personality clashes. Three or four people, maybe five, comprise a small enough cadre to know each other's work for a thorough intimate review. Once you find the match, dedicate yourself to the process.

- **The clash**. Inevitably, a clash between members will arise. And sooner or later you will be involved. Try hard to work through the controversy. No one gets through life without a bit of animosity crossing her path, and running from it hurts the group as a whole. If you've been hurt, try to step back and analyze the facts. Passion runs deep in the writing crowd. Telling someone that his words are weak or the message is unclear can sting. Work at offering criticism without barbs, even to the people who zinged your last submission. Accept criticism without scorn. Yes, someone will say something out of line along the way, but not taking issue with every remark avoids the fight.

- **The poison**. At times you find the people who poison your world. When you hate going to the group meeting it is time to analyze the benefits received versus the pain inflicted. There are people who collide with your mission. Regardless of how you behave, they take issue with you, your work, or your personality. Time to leave. Your writing becomes infected when you cannot decipher the legitimate criticism from the biting slander and jealous condescension. Crop these people out of your world or you risk eroding your writing goals and your self-esteem.

Judge the Necessity of Appearance

Before accepting an appearance of any kind, try to learn the usual tone and temperament of the event. You might decipher from a quick study just what the risk factor is for controversy and remove yourself from a potentially damaging situation. If you are shy, and shyness will not work in that setting, excuse yourself from the activity and look for other opportunities.

- **Other scheduled speakers**. Look at the biographies of the other guests. Is this a mild affair or do a couple of the speakers inflame audiences with their views and published opinions? Once a crowd is roused, it might be hard to settle them down. The marriage of you and these other speakers might not be healthy.

- **The host group**. Is the sponsoring group benign or controversial? If the members tend to have a strong opinion about any topic, assume they speak openly about their preferences. Keep your conversation gracious and middle-of-the-road or consider another event if you have serious concerns.

- **The host**. I have seen emcees of conferences that loved the limelight and treated speakers like guests at a roast. They thought it cute and humorous. You may not know the host ahead of time, but if you do and worry about the potential jabs or derailment of your appearance, ask to eliminate introductory jokes or dodge the whole affair.

- **The setting**. Are you speaking where liquor is served? Is the assembly to be held outside in ninety-degree heat? Is the audio equipment marginal? Is your signing table in front of the restroom or in the way of the general foot traffic? Know the setup plans and voice your preferences (or have your "representative" do it for you). You can learn how much respect is held for you and your work by the response and attentive behavior of the host party. If you need this gig, adapt and adjust. If you do not, then avoid it but only after you have made the effort to change the arrangements.

- **The organization**. Is this a first event or a well-established ten-year affair? While first-time events can provide more open doors for vendors, speakers, and sponsors, you have no idea how organized or financially supported the host may be. Naïve planning can lead to small speaking rooms, poor sound systems, or loose agendas, all of which have the potential to damage your image.

Calm Yourself

All of this talk about dodging, adjusting and settling. What about taking the time to calm down and deal with the situation? Know your limitations and your personal behavior. When the stress level rises a bit, have tricks in your pocket that calm you and give you focus. You might feel better later having tackled the hurtle. You read these little aids before, but as a reminder, consider:

- **Deep breaths**. Yes, they do work – one-on-one or on stage. The extra oxygen improves your thought processes and your brain loves the little kick in the pants. Shoulders tense, tongue thick, or chest tight? Find a car, restroom, outdoor spot, or corner to slow down and breathe deep. The calming effect carries you for quite a while. It evens helps control that blushing a bit.

- **Pockets**. Shaking hands distract some folks. Always wear pocketed pants or a jacket with a tissue or handkerchief inside. I have tucked comfort items in my pocket before like a coin, smooth stone, or piece of jewelry, just to have something to rub to re-center myself, and I did not realize until I wrote this book why I did it. My pockets are readily used as hiding places for my nerves.

- **Move**. Sitting or standing still allows nervous energy to bottle up, thus creating a more intense feeling. Move to dispel the energy. You can do it on stage or take a brisk walk across the parking lot, around the building, or up and down the bookstore aisles helps control those pesky agitated emotions.

- **Bathroom retreat**. Excuse yourself and gain some solitude in the restroom. Cool water on your face or neck helps. I just like the quiet and privacy, which seem to pull me back into my steady self.

- **Scream**. Others swear by it. Something about the pure release of pent up feelings lowers the pressure. I'm afraid someone will lock me up and throw away the key!

- **Sing.** If you cannot bring yourself to scream, then sing. The movement over your vocal cords has the same effect. On the way to the event, in the bathroom, outside, locked in your car with the radio turned up, sing a song you love and loosen up that voice and lower your stress level.

Shyness is a part of you. Some grow out of it, some work through it, and others live with it, chin held high. If you increasingly expose yourself to public appearances and people interaction, some of the frustration does dissipate, but the key is in the regular effort. Many of us do not get the opportunities that others do, and often the type of writing we do does not avail us to the public. Just acknowledging your shyness empowers you a bit. You entered the writing arena because you liked the words on the paper, not because you sought oral conversation. Weigh what works and what does not work for you, and balance the writing and the promotion with a middle ground that feels steady under your feet.

Character cannot be developed in ease and quiet.
Only through experience of trial and suffering can the soul be strengthened.

~Helen Keller

Chapter 12
Safe Havens and Natural Feelings

- The Shy Writer
- When Shy Equals Calm Resolve
- When Shy Equals Energy
- When Manners Speak For You
- Class and Style
- Your Safe Haven

What makes quiet and shy a good thing? Conventional wisdom suggests shyness is detrimental – but so can being gregarious. They each have a place on both the positive and negative sides of the personality fence.

Shyness appears mysterious because people cannot read it. They are unable to break down the wall to know the person, so they paint a picture of the person any way they choose. The pompous or self-enveloped person often sees shy people as less than standard. This gives him satisfaction that there is one more person beneath him that he does not have to worry about. An insecure person sees shy people as smarter – one more person that is better than she. Capitalize on these opportunities when you can – and still retain your natural quiet behavior. Consider it like playing cards. You only show what you have to in order to win the game.

The Shy Writer

Dr. Carl Jung, the famous intellect of philosophy and Freudian theory, saw introversion as a withdrawal of energy into self. But what I like about his introversion theory is that the trait is a negative reaction toward objects and appearances and a positive relationship with self and purpose. Introverts are really the ultimate people persons! They delve more into being and self-awareness than reaction to outside stimuli. In my layman's reasoning, I see the introvert as the more logical individual with a tendency toward thinking before leaping.

As a writer, being shy comes across as intellectual, literary, and introspective. The gifted artist has a reputation for being slightly anti-social anyway due to the wealth of talent and effort they channel into the art. An aura surrounds these people, and many hold them in awe. You can relate to this feeling yourself.

Marti Olsen Laney PsyD, MFT, Psychoanalyst, and author of *The Introvert Advantage: How to Thrive in an Introvert World*, lists ten advantages of the introvert. We are bright, innovative, and reliable. I love it! Feel good about these wonderful strengths and relish how your customers picture you.

- Works well with others, especially in one-to-one relationships
- Maintains long-term friendships
- Flexibility
- Independence
- Strong ability to concentrate
- Self-reflective
- Responsible
- Creative, out-of-the-box thinking
- Analytical skills that integrate complexity
- Studious and smart

As a romance author, you hold secrets about relationships, amore, feelings, and possibly even sex. You have the distinction of being envied for your sensitive feelings and understanding of human relationships. You are one enticing individual.

As a mystery writer, your mind dissects situations into question and answers. You see the world as a puzzle ever unraveling, and you keep the clues to yourself. Mystery writers are viewed as...mysterious. Readers assume you have a law, police or medical connection.

As a children's writer, you have patience and empathy for young people. You are the adult/teacher figure with a unique ability to correctly interpret a child's world at his level while infusing education and knowledge. Adults admire you for leading the next generation.

As a sci-fi writer, you live fantasy. If you seem quiet, it's only because you have a sequel in mind, and not only are you envisioning the characters, but their wardrobes, languages and modes of transportation as well. Your imagination is enviable and on "another planet" as compared to other genre writers.

As a nonfiction writer, you are the expert. Your material may cover business, pets, travel, food, fashion, families, computers, or automobiles, but you are an authority on the subject. If you are quiet, then you are contemplating your next project or solving yet another complex problem.

Of course, I made all these up. But where did I get the ideas? I have watched writers my whole life, as you may have. The chances of rubbing elbows with the rich and famous ones are slim to none – so you fantasize. And since they have published more than you have, you believe they must have something on the ball that you do not, so you give them credit for being "special." And you put names with the word "special" as I have above.

Shy writers receive labels similar to those of famous writers. If a shy writer is out of touch, readers have to establish a comfort level somewhere so they make it up. Sure, they will swear that they got the information from some article they read or interview online, but they unconsciously apply standards to the person so that the unknown no longer exists. Human beings do not like "unknown."

Bask in this glow of secrecy. Use it to your advantage. Your quiet can be construed as a calm strength and deep well of knowledge.

When Shy Equals Calm Resolve

Shyness can be a fear of speaking up or a tranquil confidence. And how is anyone to know the difference? When the fear of speaking reaches the level of not being able to speak at all to one or a hundred and one, then you need to work on the problem, possibly professionally. But when you do speak, choose your words. Say you are shy to break the ice and collect the sympathy vote of the crowd. Then give your well-planned message. As I emphasized earlier, preparedness is over half the battle against the fear of failure. As a friend once told me, "Fear is a killer. Find a 'No Fear' zone." A well-prepared individual can appear calm, cool, and collected yet be quite shy.

If your voice quivers, drink some water, soft drink, or wine to get the words flowing. Then engross yourself in your subject matter. When a quiet person delves into a subject with newfound fervor, the crowd excites and realizes that here is a person with devotion for a topic. They envy that passion that allows an introvert to step out of his shell, and they want a piece of it to take home. If you have a book, subscription or product to sell, have it readily available because at times like these, spontaneous purchases take place.

This type of shyness equals calm resolve and strength, and people admire you for it. They see a humble individual come alive with a need to express a heart-felt philosophy, and most people adore a noble cause. You overcome your own shyness to deliver an important message, and your readers want to help you succeed.

And you are not a phony in your presentation! Selling is a game. But if you feel deeply about your writing, your book, or your subject, the game becomes reality as you attempt to reach people who can benefit from your words. Who dislikes helping others? A strong emotion and personal satisfaction come with aiding others, and if your work makes someone's world happier, entertaining, easier, or gratifying, you have contributed to what we all are put on the earth to do – help our fellow man. That is empowerment personified.

When Shy Equals Energy

Shy sometimes equals nervous energy, and I confess having a history of rambling and roaming off topic due to apprehension. But remember the singers, actors and comedians in the earlier chapter? Introverted to the level of painful, these talented folks use the stage as a conduit for their feelings. Unable to bottle up their tension, they turn it into the form of drama and humor. I would crumble into a quivering mess pretending to be a character in a play. To pour that much emotion into a role before an auditorium of strangers makes me uncomfortable just thinking about it. But to comedians and actors, shyness is the catalyst to success.

If this is your presentation mode, use it! But preparation is extremely important here because lack of planning sends a nervous person on detours leading to a diluted subject. Called impromptu thinking by some, these talking nerves can undermine a your topic. An anxious chatterer wanders and allows an unexpected comment to divert attention from the matter at hand. Suddenly you are off topic seeking the steps back to your agenda.

Little tricks help keep you on task. Have a friend in the back of the room give a signal when you stray, so that you recognize the issue before it gets out of hand. Time your talks and post benchmarks on your notes. Where is the one-quarter or halfway point in your presentation? Have a clock handy with times noted in mind or even in writing on your presentation papers. I have a large clock I often take to an engagement. Posting it in the back of the room gives me constant reminder of my time constraints. Looking at a watch is considered rude in some circles.

Focusing that nervous energy into your talk with control gives the air of confidence. You do not realize how many people wish they had the drive, gusto, and intensity you do, and if you capitalize on that vitality, you come out a pure winner. People interpret your energy as passion for your subject, and, again, wish they had a piece of whatever you possess. Have those books, CDs, and subscriptions ready, because the listener wants whatever that is that makes you exciting.

When Manners Speak For You

My momma raised me to respect manners and behave in proper fashion. She taught me as I taught my family that young men open doors and hold chairs, and women thank them with a warm smile. Manners require patience and empathy, and regardless of the moment, you do not step on people to get what you want.

Competitiveness is a prerequisite to success, but enjoying the fight while casting aside your competitors is not mannerly, nor is it natural for an introvert. Healthy competition is smart use of resources, not open engagement with the enemy. Remember the gimmicks? Use them. Don't have any? Find some and have them at hand. But another tool in your box of devices is simply the strong use of your manners – otherwise known as good customer service.

The shy individual expends less energy using manners. Treating a customer like a charmed one sells a product. You have met people who were so charismatic that you felt they shut off the world to pay attention to you. Oprah Winfrey has cashed in on that trait, and that's the feeling you want to give others. Powerful energy occurs in making other people feel needed and that momentum continues when they return to their own realities.

Mark Victor Hansen, co-founder of the *Chicken Soup* series and noted "Master of Mindset," leaves an audience excited, eager and yearning to go out in to the world and accomplish great deeds. That one individual teaches others how to strive for success and measure success by the ability to help others. Marvelous message! So what happens? Everyone remembers his name and spreads the word that they want to be like him or at least live the lesson he preaches. I watched a writer online in a list group get downright silly with awe over this man. At least half a dozen writers made arrangements to attend a Hansen conference.

Make your writing mannerly and you attract more people. Believe in fairness (Angela Hoy, http://www.writersweekly.com), give back to others (Vicki Hinze, http://www.vickihinze.com), and lead with calm sincerity and respect for other human beings (Joseph Marshall III, *The Lakota Way* and *Thunderdreamer* (http://www.thunderdreamers.com), and you open big doors. Manners ring true and honest. What are some of the mannerly practices that aid you as a writer?

- **Shake hands with a firm grip**. Limp means insincerity. As a fledgling loan officer right out of college, I visited a work site to inspect collateral for a loan. The contractor took a liking to me in a fatherly way and over the next few months taught me a few basics about the working world. One of those basics was shaking a hand like I meant it. A social mannerism that speaks more than most people realize, a firm grip feels genuine, says you are glad to meet a person, and shows an interest in what he has to offer. Lack of grip signals you do not care. A hurting grip speaks intimidation. Think of it as a formal hug. A hug too tight or too fleeting means little compared to one that is just right.

- **Introduce yourself**. Even if everyone in the room knows you and your reputation, when you shake hands or greet a person, introduce yourself. Assuming everyone knows you is arrogant. And if you are afraid to greet others with your name and preferably a handshake, then you do not respect them. If they want to meet you, give them the decency of an icebreaker – your name. You might be surprised at how the other individual takes off with the conversation leaving you little to say once you break that ice.

- **Look them in the eye**. Whether talking to one or fifty, look them in the eye when you speak. Looking through them, over them, or at their shoes shows a lack of interest as if you have better things to do. I find it easier to speak to a group when I look them in the eye. I take turns with the audience members with each new thought channeled to a new pair of peepers. In individual situations, connecting eyes means listening. Try not listening while looking straight into someone's eyes. You cannot do it. Focusing on one sense usually means the others follow suit. Want to impress a publisher or agent? Grip her hand firmly, introduce yourself clearly, and look at them squarely. Your heart may be pounding in your throat, but you gain points right away. Fake it and fake it hard, if this is a struggle for you.

Class and Style

Let's see how you can say less but say more, by exuding class and style through your writing.

- **Invitations** – Generic and computer-generated invitations tend to look inexpensive and struggling. Have your logo, pen name, or identifiable design placed on invitations or note cards. Send these personal invitations not only to friends and relations, but also to dignitaries, businesses, libraries, schools, and politicians. Look at the nature of your writing and invite similar interests. The children's author may invite youth charities, law enforcement agencies, schools, and those sensitive to children's needs. The gardener needs to contact the university professor who teaches horticulture, the newspaper columnist who writes about gardening, and the nonprofit garden club who sponsors the rose show each summer. What are you inviting them to? Everything and anything. While you do not want to inundate them with all your signings, you might send them an invitation to the book fair, the literary festival, or your book release party. And if you have a string of readings, list the schedule in the invitation. Announce your book release or award. Make it personal with quality stationery that says you care.

- **Thank-yous** – Wow, the mayor did come to your booth! How did you make a note of his and other's attendance? Clearly display a sign-in book – not a spiral notebook, mind you, but a nice book resembling those at a wedding, shower or restaurant. On a carefully worded note, ask for a mailing address and email to send future notices. Assure them the information is for your use alone and not for dissemination. If they sign in, give them a pen or bookmark as a remembrance. Afterwards, send a thank-you postcard or note for doing so. Make your customers feel special. They will return it to you ten-fold. And did you note that you have not spoken a word in all of this schmoozing?

- **Newsletters** – Make them consistent and worth reading. If you do not have time to prepare one well, a reader will not have the time to read it. Too many of them swamp the Web now for you to add another mediocre letter to the emails choking everyone's mailbox. Give it an edge and keep it honed. Greet readers and thank them often. Stroke them for helping you succeed, and listen to the feedback, good and bad. You can never know it all and these readers are good educators with bright new ideas for you.

- **Emails** – Answer them quickly, with thought, and with gracious thanks for giving you the opportunity to help. Have contact information in a signature block so customers do not have to guess who you are, what you do, and where they should contact you in the future. Answer with part of the original message embedded in your reply so they remember the subject matter. Putting yourself in your customer's shoes at all times makes for pleasant business and happy acquaintances.

Your Safe Haven

No amount of fame, money and sales will make you happier than being true to yourself. So speaking pains you. Skip it and choose alternatives that gain you decent coverage like radio, press releases, gimmicks and written reviews by peers and friends. Spice up the website and throw your name all over the web.

Rumor has it that Nicholas Sparks' agent had him crash a party where the CEO of Warner Books attended. Sparks spoke to the CEO. Suddenly, the guy had a 20-city book tour. Why? The CEO liked Sparks' look. He did not have to sing and dance. He just made his own introduction and the CEO liked what he saw. Voila!

Vivia Giovannini, http://www.viviagiovannini.com, self-published *The Glass Ball* through Infinity Publishing. She prepared an exquisite promotional kit complete with bookmark, postcard, press release, professional photograph, biography, the works. I marveled at the professional look of the packet. But she confided in me her disappointment in the response rate, considering the time and expense she invested. A little later she told me that she ran into a bookstore owner who took a look at her material and offered to order some books and schedule a signing. Her press kit had landed in the wrong in-basket somewhere in his store's administrative office. She is a little lady with a little voice lacking a strong stage presence, but she sold some books to that owner just by asking if anyone had read her press release. That was a step out for her – a painless step that paid in sales. Voila again!

You will note that I chose to self-publish this book. The reasons are evident throughout these pages. I made all the right moves preached in writing manuals by talking to agents and editors who all adored *The Shy Writer* concept. Some wanted to know more and others declined my query with a "Good luck – I think it's an idea with a place. Keep trying."

I read how-to-write-book-proposal books and studied in depth how publishers want public speakers and charismatic personalities for publicity opportunities. One publisher had a four-page questionnaire with queries like:

1. Have you taught courses or given seminars?
2. Are you willing to be available for radio and TV interviews?
3. Do you know of any radio or television shows on which you might appear to discuss your book?
4. Will you need fliers for publicity events?

Yes, I could agree to do all of that – the camera, the stage and the podium. But I have a wonderful life in which I write all day and educate thousands of writers online. They email me and chat often thanking me for a step-up on their career ladder. And when I want to, I fertilize my flowers and feed the ducks on the lake behind my house. I go to the movies with my husband and play cards with my parents. As I write this, I listen to Josh Groban singing an Italian love ballad with my dachshund in my lap and a glass of Merlot on my desk. I am alone in a lovely world I am passionate about. Sometimes I laugh out loud when a fellow writer sends an instant message about the bane of writing. Other times I weep when a FundsforWriters member thanks me for opening some door in her career. But mostly I bask in my success – my ability to do what I love and enjoy life. No, I am not rich but I am financially comfortable and wealthy in that I am surrounded by what is important to me, and that is such a luxury.

I spent 25 years in a job I disliked; now I am a much better person by finding my niche as a writer. Travel on a book tour for weeks at a time would be hard on a body and a family. I have no desire to be away from home, and my family deserves better than a long-distance mom and wife. Life is so short, and they are too important. And as a person prone to a calm and quiet world, the burden of traveling promotion is too great.

Naysayers will likely tell me I chose the wrong path. And I may end up speaking at conferences that are convenient for my family. But living out of suitcases stopped a long time ago for me. I have no wish to forget the smell of the roses along my path.

Therefore, I choose a self-publishing route that touches writers via the Web. Traditionally published authors may shake their heads, but I have listened to too many of them complain about not making money until they sold book two or even three, because of promotional expense and book signings that netted five and six little sales. They hop from city to city, state to state. Been there, done that in another life. It gets old.

I do not "settle" for self-publishing as some would think. I choose the route that suits my lifestyle best. To do the book signing circuit for fewer royalties while battling a stress level that hurts my health is not living. I believe I have found a writing market I can reach without compromising myself. I believe I found my own stable, middle ground of book marketing that matches my personality.

Your goal should be to do likewise. Write your dreams and stories and poems then seek methods to market them without throwing away your soul. You cannot feel comfortable writing unless you also feel emotionally safe about the promotion.

But remember your safe haven cannot be a hideaway with no way out, either. I am the first person that would try it if it were possible. I live in my study with one eye on the computer screen and the other watching the flowers bloom. If I could converse, sell and promote 100% through the Internet, I would. But I know I might have to speak somewhere to make an impact and I will do so keeping in mind that it is good for others to hear about FundsforWriters and *The Shy Writer*. But I plan my engagements; they do not plan me.

Sometimes I enjoy outside events. I have spoken to groups where I made such a connection that time slipped through my fingers. I have arrived home exhausted from the intensity of public appearance but energized by the personalities I met. I do not speak often but not wishing to be completely reclusive, I occasionally address groups to keep me focused and to see my customers in person for a change.

My safe haven is home, but growth occurs when I test my comfort level. 'Settled and satisfied' sometimes stunts creativity and development. Staying completely hidden is not healthy, but neither is tossing your cookies five minutes before each speaking engagement. Nicholas Sparks' 20-city tour would beat some authors to death and drive them off to seclusion, but a 20-event tour around your state might suit you a little better. Or a 20-school presentation in your local region. Or a 20-club luncheon schedule close by in your hometown. Tailor your work and your promotion plan to a level that makes sales, gives you pleasure and exercises your social muscles.

The safe haven is balance, harmony, and a place where you awaken each day happy that you are a writer.

What do you like to do? If public speaking is your deal—embrace it! Go hog wild and get every speaking gig you can! If you like to hide in your skivvies behind a computer all day, well, join 2000 listservs. Find the things you enjoy doing naturally and stretch them to include your marketing efforts.

~Pari Noskin Taichert
Author, The Clovis Incident

Bibliography

Alcott, Louisa May. BrainyQuote, http://www.brainyquote.com

Ali, Mohammed. BrainyQuote, http://www.brainyquote.com

Allen, Moira. http://www.writing-world.com

Anxiety Disorder Association of America. http://www.adaa.org

Ash, Mary Kay. *Miracles Happen: The Life and Timeless Principles of the Founder of Mary Kay Inc.,* Perennial Currents, 2003.

Beoree, Dr. C. George. "Personality Theories," Shippensberg University, http://www.ship.edu/~cgboeree/perscontents.html

Brian, Cynthia. Starstyle Productions ®, Be the Star You Are ®, http://www.starstyleproductions.com http://www.bethestaryouare.org

Brice, Fanny. BrainyQuote, http://www.brainyquote.com

Bryant, Bear. *The Book of Southern Wisdom,* ed. Dr. Criswell Freeman, Walnut Grove Press, 1994.

The Burryman Writing Centre. http://www.burryman.com

Business Polish. Phoenix, Arizona, http://www.businesspolish.com

Carducci, Bernardo J., PhD. *Psychology Today,* Jan/Feb 2000.

Carver, George Washington. *The Book of Southern Wisdom,* ed. Dr. Criswell Freeman, Walnut Grove Press, 1994.

Chicken Soup for the Soul. http://www.chickensoup.com

Connelly, Michael. http://www.michaelconnelly.com

Cornwell, Patricia. The Kay Scarpetta Series,
http://www.patriciacornwell.com

Daniel, Cindy. Death Warmed Over Series,
http://www.deathwarmedovermysteries.com

Davidson, Diane Mott. Culinary Mystery Series, *Chopping Spree*
http://www.dianemottdavidson.com

Donnelly, Deborah. The Wedding Planner Series,
http://www.deborahdonnelly.org

Eleanor Roosevelt, The American Experience. Writ. Sue Williams.
With Alfre Woodard. PBS. Ambrica Productions. 2000.
http://www.pbs.org/wgbh/amex/eleanor/filmmore/description.html

Fear of Writing. www.fearofwriting.com (now changed to
http://audreyshaffer.com/chat/chat)

Gilbert, Renee, PhD. "Shake Your Shyness,"
http://www.shakeyourshyness.com

Giovannini, Vivia. *The Glass Ball,*
http://www.viviagiovannini.com

Glatzer, Jenna, *Fear is No Longer My Reality: How I Overcame
Panic and Social Anxiety and Appeared on The Bachelorette,*
http://www.jennaglatzer.com

Grafton, Sue. Author of Kinsey Millhone Series,
http://www.suegrafton.com

Halls, Kelly Milner. "Books – And Authors – for Sale,"
WritersMarket,com,
http://www.writersmarket.com/content/booksforsale.asp

Hansen, Mark Victor. "Master of Mindset,"
   http://www.markvictorhansen.com

Hart, Cassie. Cassie Hart Copywriting and Editorial Services,
   http://www.cassiehartwriter.com

Hinze, Vicki. http://www.vickihinze.com

Hood, Julie. The Organized Writer, http://organizedwriter.com

Hoy, Angela. Writers Weekly, http://www.writersweekly.com

Johnson, Lady Bird. *The Book of Southern Wisdom*, ed. Dr.
   Criswell Freeman, Walnut Grove Press, 1994.

Keller, Helen. BrainyQuotes, http://www.brainyquote.com

King, Stephen. http://www.stephenking.com

Kling, Christine. *Surface Tension*, http://www.christinekling.com

Laney, Marti Olsen, PsyD. *The Introvert Advantage: How to Thrive
   in an Extrovert World*, Workman Publishing, 2002.

Marketwire. http://www.marketwire.com

Marshall, Joseph, III. *The Lakota Way*,
   http://www.thunderdreamers.com

Martinson, Suzanne Pickett. *Outdoor Style: The Essence of
   Southwest Living*, Northland Press, 2003.
   http://www.suzannepickettmartinson.com

National Assembly of State Arts Associations.
   http://www.nasaa-arts.org

National Endowment for the Arts. http://www.nea.gov

National Institute of Mental Health. Publication NO. OM-99 4171 (Rev.), December 7, 2000.

Parlapiano, Ellen, and Cobe, Pat. *Mompreneurs: A Mother's Practical Step-By-Step Guide to Work-at-Home Success,* Perigee, 1996.

Porter, Katherine Anne. *The Book of Southern Wisdom,* ed. Dr. Criswell Freeman, Walnut Grove Press, 1994.

Press Release Writing. http://www.press-release-writing.com

PRWeb. http://www.prweb.com

Rauch, Jonathan. "Caring For Your Introvert," *Atlantic Monthly,* March 2003.

Reiss, Fern. The Publishing Game, http://www.publishinggame.com

Rice, Anne. The Vampire Chronicles, http://www.annerice.com

Rinehart, Anne. *The Bus Stop Mommies,* http://www.karenrinehart.com

Sparknotes. "Albert Einstein," Barnes & Noble, http://www.sparknotes.com/biography/einstein

Stein, Ben. World of Quotes, http://www.worldofquotes.com/author/Ben-Stein/1

Taichert, Pari Noskin. *The Clovis Incident,* http://thegreate-scape.com/parinoskintaichert

Talent Development Resources. "Introversion / Shyness," http://talentdevelop.com/introversion.html

Time Warner Bookmark. http://www.twbookmark.com

Toastmasters. http://www.toastmasters.org

Wall, Kathryn. The Bay Tanner Series,
    http://www.kathrynwall.com

WebMomz. http://www.webmomz.com

Wilson, Reid, PhD. Anxieties.com, http://www.anxieties.com

Write Success. http://www.writesuccess.com

Index

A

Absolute Write, 25
Actors, 6, 21, 23, 24, 65, 144
Agoraphobic, 25
Alcott, Louisa May, 127
Ali, Muhammad. 42
Allen, Moira. 77
Amazon, 124, 125
Anxieties.com. 131
Anxieties Disorders Association of America, 131
Ash, Mary Kay, xiv, 38
Atlantic Monthly, 8
Autoresponder, 78

B

Barry, Dave, 95
Be the Star You Are ®, *See* Brian, Cynthia
Bergman, Ingrid, 24
Blue Neon Night, See Connelly, Michael
Blushing, 64, 138, 158
Bond, James, 87
Brian, Cynthia, xi, 88
Brice, Fannie, 29
Bryant, Bear, 54
Burryman, 124
Business Polish, 85

C

Canfield, Jack, *See Chicken Soup*
Carducci, Bernardo J., 20
Carpenter, Mary Chapin, 23
Carrey, Jim, 23
Carson, Johnny, 23
Carver, George Washington, 83
Celebrations, See Michaels, Fern
Chamber of Commerce. 58. 78. 93. 121

N
NASCAR, 119
National Arts and Humanities Month, 122
National Assembly of State Arts Agencies (NASAA), 81
National Endowment for the Arts (NEA), 81
National Institute of Mental Health (NIMH), 22

O
O'Connor, Sandra Day, 50
Order Blanks, 90, 116, 126, 127
Organized Writer, See Hood, Julie
Osmond, Donny, 22
Outdoor Style: The Essence of Southwest Living, See Martinson, Suzanne

P
Panic attack, 22, 25
Parker, Peter, 4
Patterson, James, 96
Phobia, 2, 9, 36, 43, 44, 61, 131
Photo Stamps, 97
Pocket, 5, 33, 34, 61, 92, 132, 138
Poetry Society, 124
Porter, Katherine Anne, 65
Potter, Harry, 87
Press Release Writing, 103
Prime Cut, See Davidson, Diane Mott
PR Web, 103
Publishing Game, The, See Fern Reiss

Q/R
Rauch, Jonathan, 8
Reiss, Fern, 85
Rice, Anne, 86
Rickles, Don, 23
Rinehart, Karen, 119
Roberts, Nora, 86
Robb, JD, 86

Contact FundsforWriters

Learn more about the FundsforWriters family of newsletters, books, and funding information

Websites:
http://www.fundsforwriters.com
http://www.chopeclark.com
http://www.theshywriter.com

Email the author, C. Hope Clark:
hope@fundsforwriters.com

Our Newsletters

FundsforWriters – free, weekly newsletter for serious writers providing contests, markets, grants and funding information paying higher rates and royalties.

FFW Small Markets – free, weekly newsletter for serious, novice, new and seasoned writers providing contests and markets.

WritingKid – free newsletter with markets for the young writer.

TOTAL FundsforWriters – paid biweekly subscription of 90+ markets, contests, grants, publishers and jobs for the serious writer.

Read the newsletters that thousands of writers swear are the only ones they read from beginning to end!

Order Form

I would like to order the following FundsforWriters products.
I am a writer...and proud of it.

Copies   **Total**

_____   *The Shy Writer*, paperback - $ 14.95 $_____

_____   TOTAL FundsforWriters newsletter - $12 $_____

_____   FundsforWriters newsletter – FREE $__0___

_____   FFW Small Markets newsletter – FREE $__0___

_____   WritingKid newsletter – FREE $__0__

             Postage (for *The Shy Writer* only) $_____

Include $4.00 for priority mail for one copy of *The Shy Writer* (plus $1 for each additional book). $10.00 cost for international mailings.

Checks payable to: Cynthia Hope Clark

Mail:
C. Hope Clark
FundsforWriters
3145 E. Chandler Blvd Suite 110
Phoenix, AZ 85048

To place an online order or to order an electronic (ebook) version of *The Shy Writer*, go to:

http://www.theshywriter.com
http://www.fundsforwriters.com
http://www.booklocker.com

Printed in the United States
89574LV00004B/121/A